ANALYZING VIDEO SEQUENCES OF MULTIPLE HUMANS

Tracking, Posture Estimation and Behavior Recognition

THE KLUWER INTERNATIONAL SERIES IN VIDEO COMPUTING

Series Editor

Mubarak Shah, Ph.D.
University of Central Florida
Orlando, USA

Video is a very powerful and rapidly changing medium. The increasing availability of low cost, low power, highly accurate video imagery has resulted in the rapid growth of applications using this data. Video provides multiple temporal constraints, which make it easier to analyze a complex, and coordinated series of events that cannot be understood by just looking at only a single image or a few frames. The effective use of video requires understanding of video processing, video analysis, video synthesis, video retrieval, video compression and other related computing techniques.

The Video Computing book series will provide a forum for the dissemination of innovative research results for computer vision, image processing, database and computer graphics researchers, who are interested in different aspects of video.

ANALYZING VIDEO SEQUENCES OF MULTIPLE HUMANS

Tracking, Posture Estimation and Behavior Recognition

Jun Ohya
Waseda University

Akira Utsumi
Advanced Telecommunications Research Institute International

Junji Yamato
Nippon Telegraph & Telephone Corporation

KLUWER ACADEMIC PUBLISHERS
Boston / Dordrecht / London

Distributors for North, Central and South America:
Kluwer Academic Publishers
101 Philip Drive
Assinippi Park
Norwell, Massachusetts 02061 USA
Telephone (781) 871-6600
Fax (781) 681-9045
E-Mail: kluwer@wkap.com

Distributors for all other countries:
Kluwer Academic Publishers Group
Post Office Box 322
3300 AH Dordrecht, THE NETHERLANDS
Telephone 31 786 576 000
Fax 31 786 576 474
E-Mail: services@wkap.nl

Electronic Services <http://www.wkap.nl>

Library of Congress Cataloging-in-Publication Data

A C.I.P. Catalogue record for this book is available
from the Library of Congress.

Printed on acid-free paper.

Printed in the United States of America.

Contents

List of Figures ix

List of Tables xiii

Preface xvii

Contributing Authors xxi

1
Introduction 1
Jun Ohya

2
Tracking multiple persons from multiple camera images 7
Akira Utsumi

2.1 OVERVIEW 7
2.2 PREPARATION 9
2.2.1 Multiple Observations With Multiple Cameras (Observation Redundancy) 9
2.2.2 Kalman Filtering 12
2.3 FEATURES OF MULTIPLE CAMERA BASED TRACKING SYSTEM 15
2.4 ALGORITHM FOR MULTIPLE-CAMERA HUMAN TRACKING SYSTEM 17
2.4.1 Motion Tracking Of Multiple Targets 17
2.4.2 Finding New Targets 21
2.5 IMPLEMENTATION 22
2.5.1 System Overview 22
2.5.2 Feature Extraction 23
2.5.3 Feature Matching at an Observation Node 26
2.6 EXPERIMENTS 26
2.7 DISCUSSION AND CONCLUSIONS 33
Appendix: Image Segmentation using Sequential-image-based Adaptation 35

3
Posture estimation 43
Jun Ohya

3.1 Introduction 43
3.2 A Heuristic Method for Estimating Postures in 2D 46
3.2.1 Outline 46
3.2.2 Locating significant points of the human body 46
3.2.2.1 Center of Gravity of the Human Body 46
3.2.2.2 Orientation of the Upper Half of the Human Body 48
3.2.2.3 Locating Significant Points 49
3.2.3 Estimating Major Joint Positions 52
3.2.3.1 A GA Based Estimation Algorithm 52
3.2.3.2 Elbow Joint Position 53
3.2.3.3 Knee Joint Position 53
3.2.4 Experimental Results and Discussions 54
3.2.4.1 Experimental System 54
3.2.4.2 Significant Point Location Results 54
3.2.4.3 Joint Position Estimation 54
3.2.4.4 Real-time Demonstration 57
3.2.5 Summary 57
3.3 A Heuristic Method for Estimating Postures in 3D 60
3.3.1 Outline 60
3.3.2 Image Processing for Top Camera 61
3.3.2.1 Rotation Angle of the Body 61
3.3.2.2 Significant Points 63
3.3.3 Estimating Major Joint Positions 65
3.3.4 3D Reconstruction of the Significant Points 66
3.3.5 Experimental Results and Discussions 67
3.3.5.1 Experimental System 67
3.3.5.2 Significant Point Detection Results 67
3.3.6 Summary 69
3.4 A Non-heuristic Method for Estimating Postures in 3D 70
3.4.1 Outline 70
3.4.2 Locating Significant Points for Each Image 70
3.4.2.1 Contour analysis 71
3.4.2.2 The tracking process using Kalman filter and subtraction image processing 73
3.4.3 3D Reconstruction of the Significant Points 77
3.4.3.1 Front image 77
3.4.3.2 Side image 77
3.4.3.3 Top image 78
3.4.3.4 Estimating 3D coordinates 79
3.4.4 Experimental Results 79
3.4.4.1 Experimental System 79
3.4.4.2 Experimental Results 80
3.4.5 Summary 81
3.5 Applications to Virtual Environments 86
3.5.1 Virtual Metamorphosis 86
3.5.2 Virtual Kabuki System 87
3.5.3 The "Shall We Dance?" system 92
3.6 Discussion and Conclusion 94

4
Recognizing human behavior using Hidden Markov Models 99
Junji Yamato
4.1 Background and overview 99

4.2 Hidden Markov Models 102
4.2.1 Outline 102
4.2.2 Recognition 104
4.2.3 Learning 104
4.3 Applying HMM to time-sequential images 105
4.4 Experiments 108
4.4.1 Experimental conditions and pre-processes 108
4.4.2 Experiment 1 111
4.4.2.1 Experimental conditions 111
4.4.2.2 Results 111
4.4.3 Experiment 2 111
4.4.3.1 Experimental conditions 111
4.4.3.2 Results 112
4.5 Category-separated vector quantization 114
4.5.1 Problem in VQ 114
4.5.2 Category-separated VQ 114
4.5.3 Experiment 114
4.6 Applying Image Database Search 121
4.6.1 Process overview 121
4.6.2 Experiment 1: Evaluation of DCT 121
4.6.3 Experiment 2: Evaluation of precision-recall 124
4.6.4 Extracting a moving area using an MC vector 126
4.7 Discussion and Conclusion 129

5
Conclusion and Future Work 133
Jun Ohya

Index 137

List of Figures

1.1 Tracking, Posture Estimation and Behavior Recognition 2
2.1 Two-dimensional motion tracking using a one-dimensional observation 10
2.2 (A) Fully-independent observations and (B) fully-redundant observations 11
2.3 Timestamps of two-camera observations 12
2.4 (A) Most-independent observations and (B) most-redundant observations 12
2.5 Multiple-camera human tracking system 16
2.6 Observation model 17
2.7 Kalman-filtering-based matching 22
2.8 System diagram 23
2.9 Segmentation with sequential-image-based adaptation 24
2.10 Feature extraction 24
2.11 Non-synchronous observation with multiple viewpoints 25
2.12 Tracking result for one person 27
2.13 Observation intervals 27
2.14 Tracking results for two persons 28
2.15 Input image sequences (two persons) 29
2.16 Tracking accuracy for non-linear motion (circular motion) 31
2.17 Tracking results (circular motion: subject A) 32
2.18 State Tracking Result (From the top: X position, Y position, human height, and detected motion state for one person's motion) 33
2.19 Example of motion state extraction (Top: 'walking,' Middle: 'standing,' Bottom: 'sitting.' The horizontal line denotes the extracted head height.) 34
2.A.1 Hierarchical Adaptation 35
2.A.2 Coarse Segmentation 36
2.A.3 Pixel Value Distributions 37

2.A.4 Detecting Low-level Information 39

2.A.5 Segmentation using Intensity Information 40

2.A.6 Segmentation using Intensity Information 41

3.1 Posture used for the calibration 47

3.2 Example of a thermal image (gray-levels represent temperature values) 47

3.3 Distance-transformed image with a silhouette contour (gray-levels represent distance values: bright and dark levels indicate large and small values, respectively) 48

3.4 g_{ij} image with PAU (the white line) 49

3.5 Finding the temporary position of the head (the circle in this figure) 50

3.6 Local maxima of a skeleton image (white pixels) 50

3.7 Locating tip of foot 51

3.8 Contour segments to locate the tip of the hand 52

3.9 Located significant points (target images are generated by using the 3-D human body model) 55

3.10 Experimental results and reproduced Kabuki characters (left column: original thermal image; middle column: located significant points; right column: reproduction in a Kabuki avatar 56

3.11 Estimation results of an elbow joint position 58

3.12 Estimation results of a knee joint position 59

3.13 Outline of the heuristic method for 3D posture estimation 61

3.14 Principal Axis (PA) and Contour in the Top View 62

3.15 Posture for Initial Calibration in the Top View 62

3.16 Candidate for the Top of the Head in the Top View 63

3.17 Candidate for the Tip of the Foot in the Top View 64

3.18 Candidate for Hand Tip in the Top View 66

3.19 Original Trinocular Images (upper-left: front view, upper-right: side view, lower-left: top view, lower-right: no image) 68

3.20 Silhouettes of the Original Trinocular Images 68

3.21 Results of Locating Significant Points in the Trinocular Images 69

3.22 Trinocular camera system 71

3.23 Definition of $L_t - s$ curve 72

3.24 Examples of $L_t - s$ curve analysis 74

3.25 Examples of $L_t - s$ curve analysis ((a) original image, (b) contour image, (c) $L_t - s$ curve, (d) $k-$curvature, (e) $\Phi - S$ curve 75

3.26 Estimating the rotation angle using the skeleton Image in the top view 78
3.27 Examples of Estimating Postures in 3D 82
3.28 Examples of Estimating Postures in 3D 83
3.29 Examples of Estimating Postures in 3D 84
3.30 Evaluation of Estimated Positions of Left Hand 85
3.31 Virtual Kabuki System 88
3.32 Windows for Estimating Facial Expressions 89
3.33 DCT Feature Calculation 89
3.34 Changes in DCT Features and Facial Components' Shapes 90
3.35 Reference Facial Expressions Created by Artist 91
3.36 Examples of Facial Expression Reproduction 91
3.37 Scenes of the Virtual Kabuki System 92
3.38 The "Shall We Dance?" system 93
3.39 Automatic Face Tracking 94
4.1 Concept of Hidden Markov Models 103
4.2 Processing flow 106
4.3 Mesh feature 107
4.4 Sample image sequence 108
4.5 Extraction of human region 109
4.6 Extracted human images 109
4.7 Target tennis actions 110
4.8 Category separated VQ 115
4.9 Feature vector sequence in feature space 116
4.10 Code book generated from LBG Algorithm 117
4.11 Ergodic HMM and LR HMM 118
4.12 Recognition rate (1) 119
4.13 Recognition rate (2) 120
4.14 Processing flow of content-based image database retrieval using HMM behavior recognition method 122
4.15 Extracting lower frequency portion of DCT coefficients 123
4.16 Recognition rates using DCT as a feature 124
4.17 Spotting behaviors by thresholding log-likelihood 125
4.18 Precision rate and recall rate 126
4.19 Moving area extraction using MC 127
4.20 Moving area extraction using a simple threshold of MC. 128
4.21 Extracted moving areas using a combination of MC and DCT. 129
5.1 Tracking, Posture Estimation and Behavior Recognition 134

List of Tables

4.1 Likelihood (backhand volley) 112
4.2 Recognition rate (experiment 1) 112
4.3 Training patterns and test patterns 113
4.4 Recognition rate (%) (experiment 2) 113

Foreword

Traditionally, scientific fields have defined boundaries, and scientists work on research problems within those boundaries. However, from time to time those boundaries get shifted or blurred to evolve new fields. For instance, the original goal of computer vision was to understand a single image of a scene, by identifying objects, their structure, and spatial arrangements. This has been referred to as *image understanding*. Recently, computer vision has gradually been making the transition away from understanding single images to analyzing image sequences, or *video understanding*. Video understanding deals with understanding of video sequences, e.g., recognition of gestures, activities, facial expressions, etc. The main *shift* in the classic paradigm has been from the recognition of static objects in the scene to motion-based recognition of actions and events. Video understanding has overlapping research problems with other fields, therefore *blurring* the fixed boundaries.

Computer graphics, image processing, and video databases have obvious overlap with computer vision. The main goal of computer graphics is to generate and animate realistic looking images, and videos. Researchers in computer graphics are increasingly employing techniques from computer vision to generate the synthetic imagery. A good example of this is image-based rendering and modeling techniques, in which geometry, appearance, and lighting is derived from real images using computer vision techniques. Here the *shift* is from *synthesis* to *analysis followed by synthesis*. Image processing has always overlapped with computer vision because they both inherently work directly with images. One view is to consider image processing as low-level computer vision, which *processes* images, and video for later analysis by high-level computer vision techniques. Databases have traditionally contained text, and numerical data. However, due to the current availability of video in digital form, more and more databases are containing video as content. Consequently, researchers in databases are increasingly applying computer vision techniques to analyze the video before indexing. This is essentially *analysis followed by indexing*.

Due to the emerging MPEG-4, and MPEG-7 standards, there is a further overlap in research for computer vision, computer graphics, image processing, and databases. In a typical model-based coding for MPEG-4, video is first *analyzed* to estimate local and global motion then the video is *synthesized* using the estimated parameters. Based on the difference between the real video and synthesized video, the model parameters are *updated* and finally *coded* for transmission. This is essentially *analysis followed by synthesis, followed by model update, and followed by coding*. Thus, in order to solve research problems in the context of the MPEG-4 codec, researchers from different video computing fields will need to collaborate. Similarly, MPEG-7 will bring together researchers from databases, and computer vision to specify a standard set of descriptors that can be used to describe various types of multimedia information. Computer vision researchers need to develop techniques to automatically compute those descriptors from video, so that database researchers can use them for indexing.

Due to the overlap of these different areas, it is meaningful to treat *video computing* as one entity, which covers the parts of computer vision, computer graphics, image processing, and databases that are related to video. This international series on *Video Computing* will provide a forum for the dissemination of innovative research results in video computing, and will bring together a community of researchers, who are interested in several different aspects of video.

Mubarak Shah
University of Central Florida

Orlando
January 20, 2002

Preface

In recent years, **video** has become ubiquitous in daily life. The VCR has become one of the most widely used appliances, typically for recording television programs. Compact video cameras for home use are also very common. Although it has become easier to record video with such technologies, however, editing video can still be difficult or tedious for the average person (despite the development of editing software tools for the personal computer). As a result, VCR and video camera users may amass large quantities of raw, unedited footage that is seldom watched, because segments of interest to the user cannot be easily accessed. In another application, video cameras are also commonly used for surveillance of offices, shops, and homes, but these video streams may require continuous monitoring by security personnel, thus consuming valuable human resources and being prone to lapses of attention by the human observer. These examples suggest that there is a need for automatic analysis of the content of video footage (for example, to facilitate editing, retrieval, or monitoring). Such automation, ideally in real-time, would reduce the burden on the user and broaden the possible applications of video.

To pursue such goals, it is useful to take approaches from the field of **Computer Vision**, one of the most active areas of computer science, that develops algorithms to automatically analyze images acquired by cameras. Recent technical developments have enabled computer vision to deal with video sequences. Such computer vision based video analysis technologies will likely be utilized for a variety of applications, such as telecommunication, video compression, surveillance and security, advanced video games, indexing and retrieval of multimedia database systems, producing digital cinema, and editing video libraries.

This book focuses on **humans** as the subjects of video sequences. This focus is a natural consequence of the immensely important and meaningful role images of people play in daily life. Technically, video sequences of humans are a challenging target for computer vision algorithms, due to the following reasons.

- Multiple people can be in a scene at once.

- Each person may be moving.
- The human body is a 3D, non-rigid, deformable, articulated object. Therefore,
  - In a video segment a person may be in various postures, each with a dramatically different appearance.
  - Occlusions could occur. (e.g., when one body part hides another)
- Gesture and activities could vary each time they are performed, even if the subject intends to repeat the same gesture or activity.

To tackle these issues, many technologies in computer vision are needed, such as tracking, silhouette extraction, contour analysis, shape analysis, 3D reconstruction, posture estimation, and pattern recognition. Many researchers in computer vision have been attracted to these challenging problems and have been studying human image analysis. As a result of the effort made by some of the leading researchers in this area, the IEEE (Institute of Electrical and Electronics Engineers) International Conference on Face and Gesture Recognition is held every two years. This and other major computer vision conferences provide forums for presenting papers and holding discussions with researchers in this field. Thus, human image analysis is an active area in computer vision research.

It is impossible to describe all work relevant to human image analysis in this book. Therefore, we concentrate on multiple human tracking, body posture estimation, and behavior recognition. We hope that this book will be useful to our readers (some of whom may be considering or may have already undertaken related projects) and will accelerate the progress in the research areas we discuss.

JUN OHYA

Acknowledgements

First of all, the authors are very grateful that Prof. Mubarak Shah of the University of Central Florida, U.S.A. contacted Jun Ohya and encouraged him to write this book. Without Prof. Shah's proposal, suggestions, and encouragement, this book would not have been published.

The projects described in this book were developed through the efforts of many people, and were conducted in the following chronological order.

Work on behavior recognition using Hidden Markov Models (HMM) (Chapter 4) was started soon after Junji Yamato entered NTT (Nippon Telegraph & Telephone Corp., Japan) and joined J. Ohya's team in 1990. J. Yamato and J. Ohya belonged to the group led by Dr. Kenichiro Ishii, and they thank Dr. Ishii for his significant key idea of applying HMM to human behaviors in video sequences. J. Yamato thanks Shoji Kurakake (currently, at NTT DoCoMo), and Prof. Akira Tomono (currently, at Tokai University) for their contributions to the new Vector Quantization formulation. J. Yamato also thanks Dr. Hiroshi Murase of NTT for his collaboration in the application of this HMM based method to the content-based video database retrieval.

The posture estimation project (Chapter 3) was started soon after J. Ohya became the head of Department 1 of ATR (Advanced Telecommunication Research Institute) Media Integration & Communications Research Laboratories (ATR MIC), Kyoto, Japan, in 1996. Many people in Department 1 were engaged in this project. J. Ohya thanks Dr. Kazuyuki Ebihara (currently, at Japan Victor Corp.), Dr. Tatsumi Sakaguchi (currently, at Sony Corp., Japan), Prof. Jun Kurumisawa (currently, at Chiba University of Commerce, Japan), Dr. Shoichiro Iwasawa (currently, at the Telecommunications Advancement Organization of Japan), Prof. Kazuhiko Takahashi (currently, at Yamaguchi University, Japan), Masanori Yamada (currently, at NTT), Katsuhiro Takematsu (currently, at Sony Corp.) and Tetsuya Uemura (currently, at Sony Corp.) for their contributions to this project.

The human tracking project (Chapter 2) was conducted mainly by Akira Utsumi, who was a member of J. Ohya's department at ATR MIC. A. Utsumi and J. Ohya thank some student interns: Hiroki Mori (currently, at NTT), Yang Howard (currently, at University of British Columbia, Canada), Mami Kinoshita (currently, at Nagaoka University of Technology, Japan), and Hirotake Yamazoe (from Osaka University, Japan). A. Utsumi thanks Dr. Nobuji Tetsutani, the current head of Department 1 of ATR MIC for his support of this project.

J. Ohya and A. Utsumi appreciate the efforts of Dr. Ryohei Nakatsu, the director of ATR MIC, who supervised the projects described in Chapters 2 and 3. J. Ohya and A. Utsumi thank CSK Corp.'s programmers: Hiroshi Urainkyo,

Shigeo Imura and Yuji Fujimoto (currently, at Sony Corp.) for their excellent coding.

The authors would like to express their gratitude to Kluwer Academic Publishers, who allowed them to write this book. J. Ohya thanks Michael Kowalski at Brown University, U.S.A. (formerly, in J. Ohya's department at ATR MIC), who kindly edited the manuscripts for Preface, Chapter 1, Chapter 3, and Chapter 5. Finally, the authors appreciate their families' patience and cooperation during the time period in which they were intensively writing this book.

JUN OHYA, AKIRA UTSUMI, JUNJI YAMATO

Contributing Authors

Jun Ohya is a professor at the Global Information and Telecommunication Institute, Waseda University, Tokyo Japan. He got his B.S., M.S., and Ph.D. degrees in Precision Machinery Engineering from the University of Tokyo in 1977, 1979, and 1988, respectively. In 1979, he entered NTT (Nippon Telegraph & Telephone Corp) Telecommunication Laboratories and worked on full color printing technologies and computer vision related technologies. From 1988 to 1989, he was a visiting research associate of the Computer Vision Laboratory, University of Maryland, College Park, Maryland, USA. In 1992, he transferred to ATR (Advanced Telecommunications Research Institute International) Communication Systems Research Laboratories, Kyoto, Japan and worked on combining virtual reality technologies with video conferencing systems. From 1996 to 2000, he was a department head of ATR Media Integration & Communications Research Laboratories, Kyoto, Japan, and supervised research projects on computer vision, virtual reality, and computer graphics, as well as integrating art and technologies. In 2000, he joined Waseda University. His current research interest includes multimedia science based on computer vision, computer graphics, virtual reality and integration of art and technologies.

Akira Utsumi received his B.E. degree in Matallurgical Engineering from Osaka Prefecture University in 1991. He received his M.E. degree in Information & Computer Siences and his Ph.D. degree (Engineering) from Osaka University in 1993 and1999, respectively. In 1993, he joined the Communication Systems Research Laboratories at Advanced Telecommunications Research Institute International (ATR), Kyoto, Japan. From 1995 to 2001, he was with ATR Media Integration & Communications Research Laboratories. He is now a resercher at Media Information Science Laboratories at ATR. His current research interests include Computer Vision, Image Processing and Human-Computer Interaction.

Junji Yamato received B.Eng and M.Eng degrees in precision machinary engineering from the Univerisity of Tokyo, Japan, in 1988 and 1990, respectively. He received a M.S. degree in electrical engineering and computer science from the Massachusetts Institute of Technology in 1998, and a Ph.D. degree from the University of Tokyo in 2001. He was with the NTT Human Interface Laboratories, from 1990 to 1996, the MIT Artificial Intelligence Laboratory from 1996 to 1998, and the NTT Communication Science Laboratories from 1998 to 2001. He is currently a manager at the R &D strategy department of NTT Corp. His research interests include computer vision, machine learning, and human-robot interaction.

Chapter 1

INTRODUCTION

Jun Ohya
Waseda University
Global Information and Telecommunication Institute
Bldg. 29-7, 1-3-10 Nishi-Waseda, Shinjuku-ku, Tokyo 169-0051, Japan

Demand for capturing human motion has been increasing in many areas. For example, in entertainment industries that produce digital cinema and video games, human motions are measured and used for creating animations of the human body. In these applications, multiple sensing devices are attached to a human body so as to measure the movements in real-time. This contact type method is useful for fast measurement of motion data of many points on the surface of the human body. However, the contact type method is cumbersome because of the sensing devices attached to the body and the cables that connect these sensors to the controller. In telecommunication, communication methods that utilize avatars (3D human models created by computer graphics technologies) are actively being studied, where human motions are to be reproduced in the avatars. For avatar based telecommunication, capturing of human motions is very important. In fact, we developed an avatar based telecommunication system that employed the contact type method [Ohya et. al., 1995], but we encountered the above mentioned problems. In addition, the contact type method cannot be used for certain applications, such as security surveillance systems which must capture human motion in offices, shops, and at home, but without attached sensing devices. Such applications definitely require a non-contact type method, such as one based on computer vision technologies.

To capture human motion by computer vision technologies, video sequences acquired by cameras observing one or more persons are analyzed. Analyzing images of the human body in video is a challenging problem in computer vi-

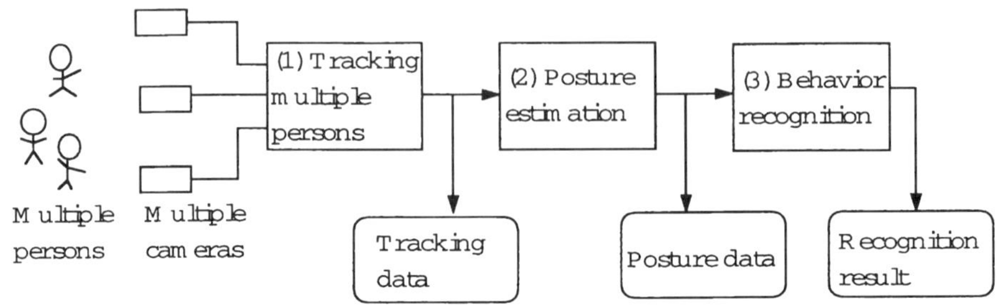

Figure 1.1. Tracking, Posture Estimation and Behavior Recognition

sion. It is due to the fact that the human body is a 3D, non-rigid, deformable, articulated object; therefore, a person can assume a variety of postures over time, with dramatic changes in appearance. Furthermore, humans can change their positions over time by walking, etc., in front of complex backgrounds that could include dynamic objects. In particular, it is difficult for computer vision algorithms to deal with occlusions that occur in video sequences (e.g., when a frontal body part occludes other body parts or when one person occludes another.)

It is impossible to describe all work relevant to human image analysis in this book. As illustrated in Fig.1.1, this book focuses on **tracking**, **posture estimation**, and **behavior recognition** as core technologies that can broaden the application areas of the non-contact type methods. These three core technologies could correspond to human visual mechanisms for perceiving a person's movements; that is, when we see a person moving, our eyes track the person; then, by analyzing the transition of postures the person assumes, our brain recognizes the person's behaviors. The blockdiagram shown in Fig.1.1 indicates that the modules for the three core technologies are sequentially connected in the order of tracking, posture estimation, and behavior recognition.

In the contact type method, the sensing devices and cables limit the area in which an individual can move, but a computer vision based method can relax this limitation and, moreover, can track more than one person simultaneously. In the tracking method described in this book, as shown in Fig.1.1, multiple persons in a scene are observed by multiple cameras and tracked regardless of occlusions. In our approach, the tracking results are sent to the posture estimation module. The tracking results can also be used by applications such as security and surveillance, which require trajectories of the persons in the scene.

The posture estimation module receives multiple tracking results and estimates the posture of each person in 3D at a given time. Like the tracking method, the posture estimation by the non-contact type method can avoid the limiatation caused by the sensors and cables. The estimated posture parameters are sent to the behavior recognition module. In the mean time, the posture data can also be used for creating animations of the human body (e.g, in entertainment applications) or for reproducing the same postures in avatar based telecommunication systems.

The behavior recognition module recognizes the multiple persons' behaviors using the time-sequneces of the estimated posture parameters as well as some other image features from the multiple cameras. The behavior recognition results are useful for applications such as the security and surveillance systems.

In this book, each of the three core technologies are explained individually. Chapters 2, 3, and 4 describe the tracking module, posture estimation module, and behavior recognition module, respectively.

Chapter 2 describes our method for tracking multiple persons by analyzing multiple video sequences [Utsumi et al., 2000]. Many computer vision based systems for tracking humans in video sequences have been proposed (e.g., [Rohr, 1994]), but self-occlusions and human-human occlusions are serious problems. To avoid these problems, multiple view camera systems have been proposed (e.g., [Gavrila et al., 1996]). These systems assume simultaneous (synchronous) observations by the multiple cameras, but synchronous systems have problems in scalability such as the redundancy in multiple observations and the need for physical mechanisms for synchronization. To eliminate these problems, our non-synchronous system described in Chapter 2 integrates the observed information using a Kalman filter based method so that dense observations with respect to the temporal axis can be obtained. The effectiveness of the non-synchronous method is shown by experimental results.

Many computer vision based methods for estimating postures of a human body have been proposed (e.g., [Horprasert et al., 1998]). As one of the most promising methods, Chapter 3 emphasizes our most recent method for locating significant points on the human body (such as the top of the head, the tips of the fingers, and the tips of the feet) in 3D in real-time [Takahashi, 2000]. Our two early systems, described in Chapter 3, estimate posture in 2D from monocular video sequece [Iwasawa et al., 1997] and in 3D from trinocular video sequences [Iwasawa et al., 2000], respectively. The methods used heuristic rules and empirical knowledge about the human body; in contrast, our most recent 3D posture esitmation method utilizes a function based algorithm that analyzes contour curvature of the human silhouettes so that the heuristic rules and empirical knowledge need not be used. In addition, the most recent system can cope with self-occlusions by exploiting a Kalman filter based tracking algorithm and image difference. The methods described in Chapter 3 are successfully applied to some avatar based telecommunication systems.

Chapter 4 describes our work for recognizing human behaviors from time-sequential images using HMMs (Hidden Markov Models) [Yamato et al., 1992]. HMMs have been succesfully applied to speech recognition, but for the first time, we showed that HMMs are useful also for computer vision based recognition of human behaviors from video sequences. Our work on HMMs is highly cited. In Chapter 4, specific details about the learning and recognition procedures such as converting image feature sequences to symbol sequences using Vector Quantization are explained. Experimental results using tennis action data demonstrate the effectiveness of the method.

Chapter 5 concludes this book with discussion and future research.

References

Gavrila, D.M. and Davis, L.S. (1996). 3-d model-based tracking of humans in action: a multi-view approach. In *Proc. of IEEE Computer Society Conference on Computer Vision and Pattern Recognition*, pages 73–80.

Horprasert, T., Haritaoglu, I., Wren, C., Harwood, D., Davis, L.S., and Pentland, A. (1998). Real-time 3D motion capture. In *Proc. of 1998 Workshop on Perceptual User Interface*, pages 87–90.

Iwasawa, S., Ebihara, K., Ohya, J., and Morishima, S. (1997). Real-time estimation of human body posture from monocular thermal images. In *Proc. of 1997 IEEE Computer Society Conference on Computer Vision and Pattern Recognition*, pages 15–20.

Iwasawa, S., Ohya, J., Takahashi, K., Sakaguchi, T., Ebihara, K., and Morishima, S. (2000). Human body postures from trinocular camera images. In *Proc. of Fourth IEEE International Conference on Automatic Face and Gesture Recognition*, pages 326–331.

Ohya, J., Kitamura, Y., Takemura, H., Ishii, H., Kishino, F. and Terashima, N. (1995). Virtual Space Teleconferencing: Real-time reproduction of 3D human images *Journal of Visual Communication and Image Representation*, 6 (1) : 1–25.

Rohr, K. (1994). Towards model-based recognition of human movements in image sequences. *Computer Vision, Graphics, and Image Processing: Image Understanding*, 59(1):94–115.

Takahashi, K., Sakaguchi, T., and Ohya, J. (2000). Remarks on a real-time 3D human body posture estimation method using trinocular images. In *Proc. of 15th International Conference on Pattern Recognition*, 4:693–697.

Utsumi, A. and Ohya, J. (2000). Multiple-camera-based human tracking using non-synchronous observations. In *Proc. of Asian Conference on Computer Vision*, pages 1034–1039.

Yamato, J., Ohya, J., and Ishii, K. (1992) Recognizing human action in time-sequential images using Hidden Markov Models. In *Proc. of IEEE Com-*

puter Society Conference on Computer Vision and Pattern Recognition, pages 379–387.

Chapter 2

TRACKING MULTIPLE PERSONS FROM MULTIPLE CAMERA IMAGES

Akira Utsumi
Advanced Telecommunications Research Institute International,
2-2-2 Hikaridai, Seikacho, Sorakugun Kyoto 619-0288, Japan

Abstract This chapter discusses a human tracking method using multiple non-synchronous camera observations. In vision-based human tracking, self-occlusions and human-human occlusions are significant problems. Employing multiple view-points reduces these problems. Furthermore, the use of the non-synchronous observation approach eliminates the scalability problem inherent in synchronous systems. In the system described in this chapter, each camera independently observes a scene and thus does not require any special synchronization mechanism. The multiple observations are integrated with a Kalman-filter-based algorithm. With its non-synchronous approach, the system can obtain dense observations for the temporal axis, and the total performance is not affected by increasing the number of cameras. We developed the experimental system to accommodate five or more cameras. The system can track human positions in both single-person and multiple-person situations. Experimental results show the effectiveness of the non-synchronous multiple-camera system.

Keywords: Human tracking, multiple-camera system, non-synchronous observations, Kalman filtering

2.1. OVERVIEW

Human motion tracking using computer vision techniques is becoming an active research field. Many vision-based systems for detecting and tracking human motion information have already been proposed [Rohr, 1994; Yamamoto and Koshikawa, 1991; O'Rourke and Badler, 1980; Azarbayejani and Pentland, 1996; Wren et al., 1996; Johnson et al., 1994; Segen and Pingali, 1996; Khan and Shah, 2000]. Most of these systems deal with the 3-D tracking of human movements. The most common applications include man-machine interfaces using body movements, remote surveillance systems, and so on.

Vision systems, however, still have several limitations in both robustness and scalability. In this chapter, we introduce a multiple-viewpoint system to reduce these problems.

Stereo is the most commonly used mechanism to extract 3-D information in a vision system. Stereo is also the basis for 3-D object tracking. Matthies et al. installed a stereo system on a robot arm and moved the arm to retrieve self-locations in 3-D [Matthies and Shafer, 1987]. Yi et al. used a stereo system and proposed a robust mechanism to match the detected 3-D points in a time sequence [Yi and Oh, 1997]. Yi et al. also used a Kalman filter to integrate sequential information. Naturally these stereo systems are based on two viewpoints.

In human motion tracking tasks, a restricted number of cameras in the system can cause frequent problems. Humans tend to move around within a wide area, so it is difficult to cover any one area with a small number of cameras. With multiple persons, one person can easily occlude another, making accurate tracking difficult. To avoid these problems, a multiple-viewpoint approach is useful. A multiple-viewpoint system can cover a wide area and compensate for occlusion with its multiple cameras [Gavrila and Davis, 1996; Cai and Aggarwal, 1996; Utsumi et al., 1998; Nakazawa et al., 1998].

Most multiple-viewpoint systems assume simultaneous camera observations and detect 3-D points for each set of observations. The matching process among the cameras is simplified via the simultaneous observations because the correlations are maximized among the images. However, it is still necessary to have correspondences between succeeding frames since the camera observations are essentially discrete for the temporal axis.

Synchronous systems also have problems in scalability. First, the total performance (system throughput) becomes worse with an increasing number of cameras because the slowest image process determines the total throughput. Second, the redundancy among multiple observations increases with the number of cameras used because all observations happen at the same time. Third, a special physical mechanism (i.e., the distribution of synchronization signals) is necessary to guarantee synchronization among the cameras. This often becomes a serious burden, especially when the cameras are very far apart (for instance, when tracking a sports event with distributed cameras).

To overcome these disadvantages, we propose a system that implements a non-synchronized observation method. Our system does not require any synchronization mechanism. In a practical implementation, the observed information is integrated based on Kalman filtering. In our method, the performance of each camera observation is not affected by increasing the number of cameras because each image processing runs independently of the other processes. As the observations in the multiple viewpoints are fully random, the redundancy among the multiple observations can be reduced and the system can obtain dense observations for the temporal axis.

In this chapter, the next section discusses observation redundancy in multiple-camera systems and introduces a Kalman filtering algorithm. Section 2.3 shows a brief sketch of our human tracking system. Section 2.4 provides details of our tracking algorithm. Section 2.5 describes how the algorithm is implemented and gives details on the image processing. Section 2.6 gives experimental results. Section 2.7 concludes this chapter.

2.2. PREPARATION

In this section, as preparation for understanding the later sections, we briefly discuss the issue of redundancy among observations, which is a significant factor in multiple-camera systems. In a multiple-camera system, we have to deal with many more observations than in a single (or conventional stereo) camera system. To make these observations truly useful, we have to carefully consider the observation conditions. Observation redundancy is one of the key issues to examine.

It is also important to find a method capable of integrating a large number of observations effectively. This section gives a brief introduction to the Kalman filtering algorithm used for integrating multiple observations in our human tracking system.

2.2.1. Multiple Observations With Multiple Cameras (Observation Redundancy)

In multiple-camera-based tracking systems, a number of cameras observe the motion of a single target or multiple targets from similar or totally different viewpoints. The target object(s) can appear to move around within the scene and to disappear from the scene. Obviously, the situation surrounding the cameras and target(s) is very diverse and can easily change from time to time. Accordingly, the observation conditions can be different for each observation, and the reliability of the information given by each observation can also vary. We therefore need an effective mechanism to integrate the observed information.

On the other hand, to achieve stable tracking, we need a variety of observation conditions. For instance, by using the observations of different viewpoints, we can reduce the chances of mutual occlusion and self-occlusion (singular view). To obtain more information from the same number of observations, we should have less redundant (different-conditioned) observations. Unfortunately, with a large number of cameras, redundant (similar-conditioned) observations can easily occur. Therefore, we have to be aware of redundancy issues when designing an effective tracking system. Here, we consider two types of redundancies: spatial redundancies and temporal redundancies.

Spatial (Viewpoint) Redundancy As an example, we discuss the redundancy among observations from different viewpoints for position estimation.

Let us consider the case of a 1-D observation of a 2-D scene (Fig. 2.1). Two cameras, camera 1 and camera 2, observe a target object. θ_1 and θ_2 are the angles between the Y axis and the target projection line for each camera's observation. $\theta_1 - \theta_2$ denotes the angle between the two observations. Here, we do not consider any difference in the observation errors for the view directions. The target position can be determined as the crosspoint of the two projection lines with a certain amount of observation errors.

Now, we can imagine two extreme cases. The first one is where the two observations are totally orthogonal ($\theta_1 - \theta_2 = \pi$). For instance, for $\theta_1 = \pi$ and $\theta_2 = 0$, the target information given by camera 1 only regards the Y direction. On the other hand, camera 2 only gives information on the X direction (Fig. 2.2(A)). This means that the information of one observation is fully independent of that of the other observation (not redundant at all) and that the total information on the target position given by the two observations becomes maximum.

The second case is where the two cameras have the same direction as the target (for instance, both θ_1 and θ_2 are 0) (Fig. 2.2(B)). In this case, the infor-

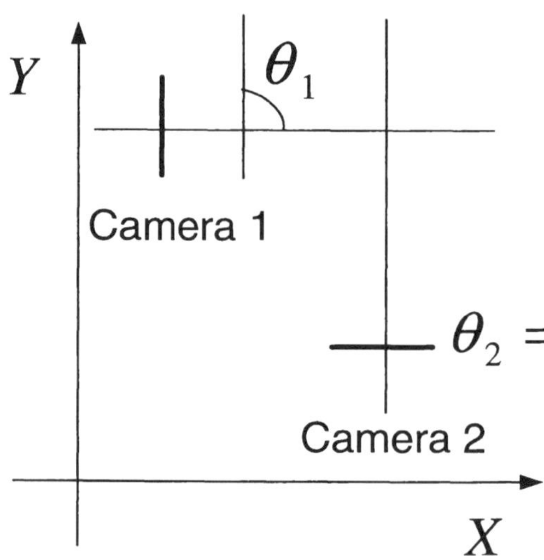

Figure 2.1. Two-dimensional motion tracking using a one-dimensional observation

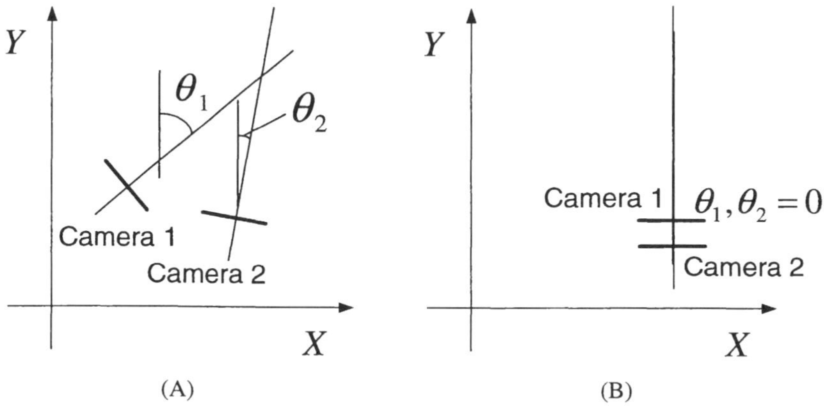

Figure 2.2. (A) Fully-independent observations and (B) fully-redundant observations

mation from the two cameras will be identical except for the observation errors. As a result, the two observations will be highly redundant. No information in the Y direction can be obtained from these observations.

Observations are generally somewhere between these two extreme cases. To retrieve more information from a fixed number of observations, less redundant observations are desirable. Of the above cases, case (A) is the most desirable as long as the target can be identified in images.

Temporal Redundancy Since the tracking process detects the target state not only in the spatial axis but also in the temporal axis, observation redundancy can also occur in the temporal axis.

Let us consider the case of observations with two cameras. Here, we assume the same observation conditions for both cameras. Each camera observes the scene iteratively at a constant interval of Δt, in the same way as a conventional video camera. Figure 2.3 shows the situation. Here, an observation is first made by camera 1 at t_1. Then, the next observation is made by camera 2 at t_2. $t_2 - t_1$ denotes the time between the two observations.

Again, we consider two extreme cases. The first one is when the two cameras are synchronized ($t_2 - t_1 = 0$) (Fig. 2.4(B)). In this case, the target is observed every Δt, and the observations in the temporal axis become most sparse. The two observations become most redundant because of the common target state.

On the other hand, the observations become most dense in the temporal axis when the two observations are farthest apart (i.e., $t_2 - t_1 = \Delta/2$) (Fig. 2.4(A)). As the states of the target (position, velocity, etc.) are always changing, a dense observation has a greater chance of detecting the changes immediately. In other words, a less redundant observation is desirable for getting more information.

In our human tracking system, we aim at obtaining a variety of observations, not only spatially but also temporally.

To utilize the less redundant observations effectively, we need a mechanism to integrate the observed data. We employ a Kalman filtering algorithm to integrate multiple observations. In the next section, we briefly introduce the Kalman filtering algorithm.

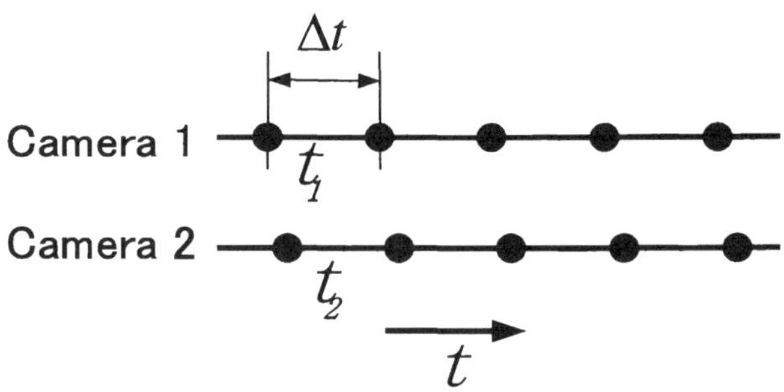

Figure 2.3. Timestamps of two-camera observations

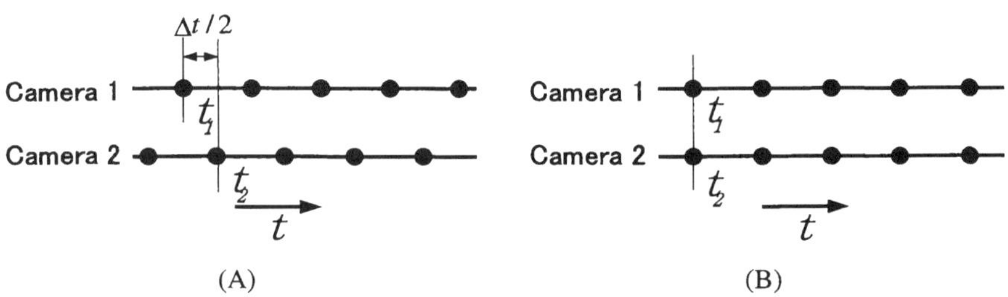

Figure 2.4. (A) Most-independent observations and (B) most-redundant observations

2.2.2. Kalman Filtering

The Kalman filter is a state estimation algorithm for dynamic systems proposed by Kalman et al. in 1960 [Kalman, 1960]. It describes the target system as a linear system and assumes Gaussian white noise as both the process noise and measurement errors. The total algorithm can be considered an extension of the minimum mean square estimation to a dynamic process.

Here, we will briefly introduce the Kalman filter for discrete systems used in the following sections. The explanation here is based on a MAP estimation framework.[1]

Linear System Let the state of a system at time t be described as an n-dimensional stochastic vector $\boldsymbol{X}_t$. The state of this system at time $t+1$ can be estimated with the following state transition equation.

$$\boldsymbol{X}_{t+1} = \boldsymbol{F}\boldsymbol{X}_t + \boldsymbol{w}_t, \tag{2.1}$$

where, $\boldsymbol{F}$ is an $n \times n$ transition matrix and $\boldsymbol{w}_t$ is an n-dimensional Gaussian noise vector in the transition (the covariance matrix of $\boldsymbol{w}_t$ is $\boldsymbol{R}_t$).

We express the estimation of the state vector $\boldsymbol{X}$ at time t with a Gaussian distribution. Let the average be $\bar{\boldsymbol{X}}_t$ and the covariance matrix be $\boldsymbol{P}_t$.

Then, the estimations of $\boldsymbol{X}$ at time $t+1$ can be calculated from equation (2.1) as follows.

$$\hat{\boldsymbol{X}}_{t+1} = \boldsymbol{F}\bar{\boldsymbol{X}}_t, \tag{2.2}$$

$$\boldsymbol{M}_{t+1} = \boldsymbol{F}\boldsymbol{P}_t\boldsymbol{F}' + \boldsymbol{R}_t, \tag{2.3}$$

where $\hat{\boldsymbol{X}}_{t+1}$ and $\boldsymbol{M}_{t+1}$ are the average and covariance matrix of the estimation, respectively.

Accordingly, the probability of occurrence $\boldsymbol{X}$ at time $t+1$ is given as follows.

$$\begin{aligned} P(\boldsymbol{X}_{t+1}) &= (2\pi)^{-n}|\boldsymbol{M}_{t+1}|^{-\frac{1}{2}} \\ &\quad \exp\left\{-\frac{1}{2}(\boldsymbol{X}_{t+1} - \bar{\boldsymbol{X}}_{t+1})'\boldsymbol{M}_{t+1}^{-1}(\boldsymbol{X}_{t+1} - \bar{\boldsymbol{X}}_{t+1})\right\}. \end{aligned} \tag{2.4}$$

Measurement (Observation) Equations (2.2) and (2.3) give an estimation of $\boldsymbol{X}$ based on past information. To reduce ambiguity and update the estimation, we have to measure $\boldsymbol{X}$ somehow. The next equation denotes a measurement at time $t+1$.

$$\boldsymbol{z}_{t+1} = \boldsymbol{H}\boldsymbol{X}_{t+1} + \boldsymbol{v}_{t+1}, \tag{2.5}$$

where, $\boldsymbol{H}$ is an $m \times n$ measurement matrix and $\boldsymbol{z}$ is an observed m-dimensional vector. We also consider Gaussian noise in this process. $\boldsymbol{v}_{t+1}$ is an m-dimensional noise vector and $\boldsymbol{Q}_{t+1}$ is the covariance of $\boldsymbol{v}_{t+1}$.

Updating State Estimation When $\boldsymbol{X}_{t+1}$ follows the Gaussian distribution shown in (2.4) (i.e., average $\bar{\boldsymbol{X}}_{t+1}$ and covariance $\boldsymbol{M}_{t+1}$), then the measurement vector $\boldsymbol{z}_{t+1}$ is expected to follow a Gaussian distribution with average $\bar{\boldsymbol{z}}_{t+1}$ and covariance $\boldsymbol{S}_{t+1}$, which are estimated as follows.

$$\bar{\boldsymbol{z}}_{t+1} = \boldsymbol{H}\bar{\boldsymbol{X}}_{t+1}, \tag{2.6}$$

$$\boldsymbol{S}_{t+1} = \boldsymbol{H}\boldsymbol{M}_{t+1}\boldsymbol{H}' + \boldsymbol{Q}_{t+1}. \tag{2.7}$$

Accordingly, the probability distribution of $\boldsymbol{z}_{t+1}$ can be calculated as follows.

$$P(\boldsymbol{z}_{t+1}) = (2\pi)^{-m}|\boldsymbol{S}_{t+1}|^{-\frac{1}{2}} \exp\left\{-\frac{1}{2}(\boldsymbol{z}_{t+1} - \bar{\boldsymbol{z}}_{t+1})'\boldsymbol{S}_{t+1}^{-1}(\boldsymbol{z}_{t+1} - \bar{\boldsymbol{z}}_{t+1})\right\}. \tag{2.8}$$

On the other hand, if the state $\boldsymbol{X}_{t+1}$ is known, $P(\boldsymbol{z}_{t+1}|\boldsymbol{X}_{t+1})$, which is the probability distribution of $\boldsymbol{z}_{t+1}$ under the condition $\boldsymbol{X}_{t+1}$, can be written as follows.

$$\begin{aligned} P(\boldsymbol{z}_{t+1}|\boldsymbol{X}_{t+1}) &= (2\pi)^{-m}|\boldsymbol{Q}_{t+1}|^{-\frac{1}{2}} \exp\{ \\ & -\frac{1}{2}(\boldsymbol{z}_{t+1} - \boldsymbol{H}\boldsymbol{X}_{t+1})'\boldsymbol{Q}_{t+1}^{-1}(\boldsymbol{z}_{t+1} - \boldsymbol{H}\boldsymbol{X}_{t+1})\}. \end{aligned} \tag{2.9}$$

From equations (2.4), (2.8) and (2.9), the probability distribution of $\boldsymbol{X}_{t+1}$ under the observation $\boldsymbol{z}_{t+1}$ can be calculated as follows by using the Bayes rule.

$$P(\boldsymbol{X}_{t+1}|\boldsymbol{z}_{t+1}) = \frac{P(\boldsymbol{X}_{t+1})P(\boldsymbol{z}_{t+1}|\boldsymbol{X}_{t+1})}{P(\boldsymbol{z}_{t+1})} \tag{2.10}$$

$\bar{\boldsymbol{X}}_{t+1}$, the updated estimation of $\boldsymbol{X}$ under the measurement $\boldsymbol{z}_{t+1}$, is determined as the $\boldsymbol{X}$ that maximizes the above equation. Consequently, it gives the following result.

$$\bar{\boldsymbol{X}}_{t+1} = \hat{\boldsymbol{X}}_{t+1} + \boldsymbol{K}_{t+1}\left(\boldsymbol{z}_{t+1} - \boldsymbol{H}\hat{\boldsymbol{X}}_{t+1}\right). \tag{2.11}$$

$\boldsymbol{K}_{t+1}$ is called the 'Kalman gain' and expressed as the following equation.

$$\boldsymbol{K}_{t+1} = \boldsymbol{P}_{t+1}\boldsymbol{H}\boldsymbol{Q}_{t+1}^{-1}. \tag{2.12}$$

Here,

$$\boldsymbol{P}_{t+1} = \left(\boldsymbol{M}_{t+1}^{-1} + \boldsymbol{H}'\boldsymbol{Q}_{t+1}^{-1}\boldsymbol{H}\right)^{-1}. \tag{2.13}$$

According to equation (2.11), we can update the state vector for every observation z_t.

The filtering process is achieved by repeating the above manipulations (2.2), (2.3), and (2.11)–(2.13).

2.3. FEATURES OF MULTIPLE CAMERA BASED TRACKING SYSTEM

In the previous section, we discussed redundancy issues in multiple-viewpoint systems and introduced the Kalman filtering algorithm. Our system integrates multiple non-synchronous observations by using the Kalman filter and performs human motion tracking. In this section, as a prelude to introducing our tracking algorithm in the next section, we summarize the following features of our human tracking system.

- Multiple-Camera System
- Distributed Processing
- Non-Synchronous Observations
- Kalman Filter Based Tracking

Multiple-Camera System By using multiple cameras, we can observe a scene in many directions and from many viewpoints (Figure 2.5). This means that we can reduce the chances of occlusion and easily expand the detection area. In addition, by integrating the observations from the multiple viewpoints, we can achieve more reliable and accurate tracking results.

Distributed Processing Image processing generally requires high computation costs (power and computation time). This often becomes a significant problem in multiple-camera systems because a large number of images must be processed. Our system solves this problem by employing fully distributed processing. In our system, each camera image is processed by a local processor (observation node). We process one camera image with one processor (computer). In addition, two other processors are used for the tracking process (tracking node) and the target-finding process (discovering node). A normal computer network is used for all communications among the observation nodes, tracking node, and discovering node. As all 2-D image processing is performed locally at each observation node, the amount of information exchanged through the network is limited to a trivial amount of information such as 2-D positions of image features, observation times, and so on. Consequently, the communications overhead is not significant.

Non-Synchronous Observations In our system, each observation node observes a scene without any synchronization. This feature makes it possible to reduce the redundancy among multiple observations (discussed in the previous section) and to more efficiently detect the fraction of the target motion in the temporal axis. In addition, non-synchronous observations also have several benefits for implementation. In particular, we do not need any mechanism for synchronization. This is especially useful when the observation nodes are placed very far apart. Furthermore, we do not need to be concerned about the processing speed of each observation node. Generally, the processing time for one image can vary depending on the content of the image as well as on the performance of the processor used for the observation node. By employing non-synchronous observations, however, each observation node can work based on its own processing speed and the content of the image.

Kalman Filter Based Tracking As described in the previous section, we employ the Kalman filtering algorithm to integrate the non-synchronous multiple-

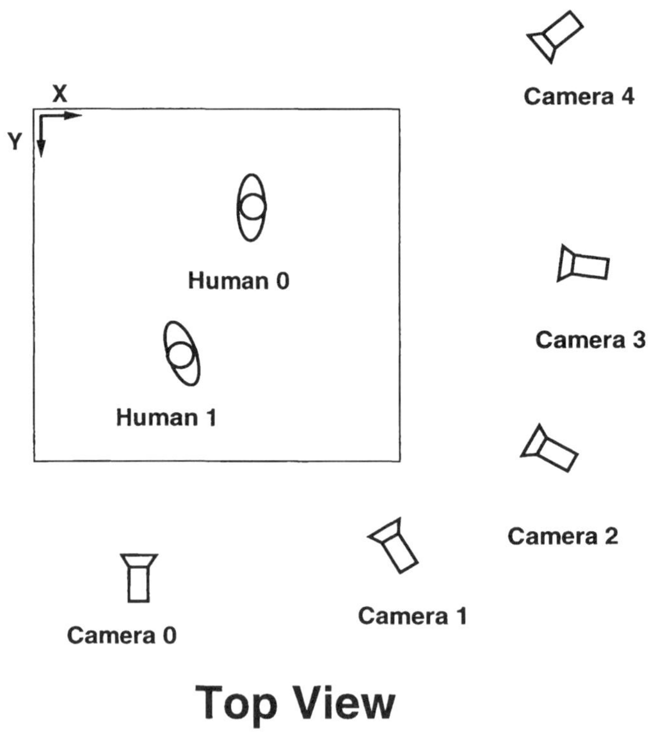

Figure 2.5. Multiple-camera human tracking system

viewpoint observations of the system. Each piece of observed information is sent to the tracking node with a time-stamp of its observation and is integrated into the tracking model for every single observation. By using this method, we can develop a system that is scalable for both the number of cameras and the performance capability of each observation node.

In the next section, we describe our algorithm in detail.

2.4. ALGORITHM FOR MULTIPLE-CAMERA HUMAN TRACKING SYSTEM

2.4.1. Motion Tracking Of Multiple Targets

Observation Model Figure 2.6 shows our observation model for one camera. Though a camera can observe multiple targets, we concentrate on a one-target case to simplify the explanation. This explanation can easily be extended to multiple-target cases.

Let us consider the target object h_j located at $\boldsymbol{X}_{x_j,t_n}$ $(= (X_{j,t_n}, Y_{j,t_n}))$ at time t_n projected onto the image plane of the i-th camera at $\boldsymbol{C}_i$. Here, φ_{ij,t_n} is the angle between the target projection line $\boldsymbol{X}_{x_j,t_n} - \boldsymbol{C}_i$ and the Y-axis. $\boldsymbol{R}_{\varphi_{ij,t_n}}$ denotes the rotation matrix that rotates the projection line so that it is parallel to the Y-axis.

Accordingly, we express one observation as $\boldsymbol{z}_{x_j,t_n}$.

$$\boldsymbol{z}_{x_j,t_n} = \boldsymbol{H}_x \boldsymbol{R}^{-1}_{\varphi_{ij,t_n}} \boldsymbol{X}_{x_j} + \boldsymbol{v}_{x_j,t_n}. \tag{2.14}$$

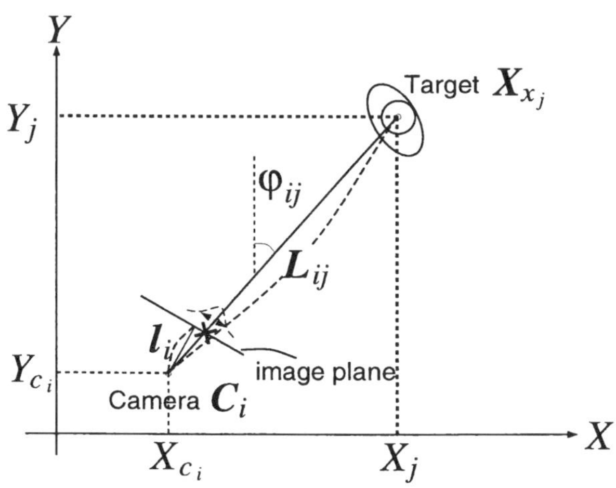

Figure 2.6. Observation model

Here,

$$\boldsymbol{H}_x = \begin{bmatrix} 1 & 0 \\ 0 & 0 \end{bmatrix}. \tag{2.15}$$

$\boldsymbol{v}_{x_j,t_n}$ is the measurement error (average $\boldsymbol{0}$, covariance matrix $\boldsymbol{Q}_{x_j,t_n}$). The size of the measurement error increases with the distance from the observing camera. We express the error size as follows.

$$\boldsymbol{Q}_{x_j,t_n} = \frac{\bar{L}_{ij,t_n}}{l_i}\boldsymbol{Q}_0 \simeq \frac{L_{ij,t_n}}{l_i}\boldsymbol{Q}_0, \tag{2.16}$$

where L_{ij,t_n} is the distance between the target h_j and camera i, and l_i is the focal length of camera i. We approximate the distance with $\bar{L}_{ij,t_n}$ (the distance between $\boldsymbol{C}_i$ and $\bar{\boldsymbol{X}}_{x_j,t_n}$) instead of L_{ij,t_n} because the actual distance L_{ij,t_n} is not applicable. $\boldsymbol{Q}_0$ denotes the standard level of the error covariance.

In practice, $\boldsymbol{z}_{x_j,t_n}$ in equation (2.14) is calculated from φ_{ij,t_n}, which is determined by an observation and camera position $\boldsymbol{C}_i$ as follows.

$$\boldsymbol{z}_{x_j,t_n} = \boldsymbol{H}\boldsymbol{R}^{-1}_{\varphi_{ij,t_n}}\boldsymbol{C}_i. \tag{2.17}$$

Furthermore, the target object is considered to have physical properties that can be observed as image features (body height, cloth color, etc.). Here, we express the properties for the target h_j as $\boldsymbol{X}_{s_j}$, which are observed as $\boldsymbol{z}_{s_j}$ in images. This observation is expressed as follows.

$$\boldsymbol{z}_{s_j,t_n} = \boldsymbol{H}_s\boldsymbol{X}_{s_j,t_n} + \boldsymbol{v}_{s_j,t_n}, \tag{2.18}$$

where $\boldsymbol{v}_{s_j,t_n}$ expresses the observation error in the same way as $\boldsymbol{v}_{x_j,t_n}$ in (2.14) (the covariance matrix is $\boldsymbol{Q}_s$).

Target Motion Assuming a constant velocity for the target motion, the geometrical state of the target can be expressed as $[\ \boldsymbol{X}'_{x_j} \quad \dot{\boldsymbol{X}}'_{x_j}\ ]'$. Here, $\dot{\boldsymbol{X}}_{x_j}$ expresses the target's velocity vector. Therefore, the state change in a small time difference can be described as follows.

$$\begin{bmatrix} \boldsymbol{X}_{x_j,t_{n+1}} \\ \dot{\boldsymbol{X}}_{x_j,t_{n+1}} \end{bmatrix} = \boldsymbol{F}_x \begin{bmatrix} \boldsymbol{X}_{x_j,t_n} \\ \dot{\boldsymbol{X}}_{x_j,t_n} \end{bmatrix} + \Delta t \cdot \boldsymbol{w}_{x_j,t_n}, \tag{2.19}$$

where

$$\Delta t = t_{n+1} - t_n. \tag{2.20}$$

The transition matrix $\boldsymbol{F}_x$ is as follows.

$$\boldsymbol{F}_x = \begin{bmatrix} 1 & 0 & \Delta t & 0 \\ 0 & 1 & 0 & \Delta t \\ 0 & 0 & 1 & 0 \\ 0 & 0 & 0 & 1 \end{bmatrix}. \tag{2.21}$$

In equation (2.19), $\boldsymbol{w}_{x_j,t_n}$ expresses the fluctuation of the geometrical state for a unit of time (its covariance matrix is $\boldsymbol{R}_x$).

If the distribution of $[\ \boldsymbol{X}'_{x_j,t_n} \quad \dot{\boldsymbol{X}}'_{x_j,t_n}\ ]'$ at t_n is given, then the estimation of $\boldsymbol{X}_{x_j}$ and $\dot{\boldsymbol{X}}_{x_j}$ at t_{n+1} can be calculated. Let the average and the covariance matrix of the estimation of $[\ \boldsymbol{X}'_{x_j,t_n} \quad \dot{\boldsymbol{X}}'_{x_j,t_n}\ ]'$ be $[\ \bar{\boldsymbol{X}}'_{x_j,t_n} \quad \bar{\dot{\boldsymbol{X}}}'_{x_j,t_n}\ ]'$ and $\boldsymbol{P}_{x_j,t_n}$, respectively. Then, the estimation of $\boldsymbol{X}_{x_j}$ and $\dot{\boldsymbol{X}}_{x_j}$ at t_{n+1} can be calculated as follows.

$$\begin{bmatrix} \hat{\boldsymbol{X}}_{x_j,t_{n+1}} \\ \hat{\dot{\boldsymbol{X}}}_{x_j,t_{n+1}} \end{bmatrix} = \boldsymbol{F}_x \begin{bmatrix} \bar{\boldsymbol{X}}_{x_j,t_n} \\ \bar{\dot{\boldsymbol{X}}}_{x_j,t_n} \end{bmatrix}, \tag{2.22}$$

$$\boldsymbol{M}_{x_j,t_{n+1}} = \boldsymbol{F}_x \boldsymbol{P}_{x_j,t_n} \boldsymbol{F}'_x + \Delta t \cdot \boldsymbol{R}_{x_j,t_n}, \tag{2.23}$$

where $[\ \hat{\boldsymbol{X}}'_{x_j,t_{n+1}} \quad \hat{\dot{\boldsymbol{X}}}'_{x_j,t_{n+1}}\ ]'$ is the the average of the estimation at t_{n+1} and $\boldsymbol{M}_{x_j,t_{n+1}}$ is its covariance matrix.

Similarly, we consider the transition of physical properties $\boldsymbol{X}_{s_j}$ in a time sequence as follows.

$$\boldsymbol{X}_{s_j,t_{n+1}} = \boldsymbol{X}_{s_j,t_n} + \Delta t \cdot \boldsymbol{w}_{s_j,t_n}, \tag{2.24}$$

where $\boldsymbol{w}_{s_j,t_n}$ denotes the transition fluctuation of the physical properties (its covariance is $\boldsymbol{R}_s$).

The estimation for this transition can be given as follows.

$$\hat{\boldsymbol{X}}_{s_j,t_{n+1}} = \bar{\boldsymbol{X}}_{s_j,t_n}, \tag{2.25}$$

$$\boldsymbol{M}_{s_j,t_{n+1}} = \boldsymbol{P}_{s_j,t_n} + \Delta t \cdot \boldsymbol{R}_{s_j,t_n}, \tag{2.26}$$

where $(\bar{\boldsymbol{X}}_{s_j,t_n}, \boldsymbol{P}_{s_j,t_n})$ and $(\hat{\boldsymbol{X}}_{s_j,t_{n+1}}, \boldsymbol{M}_{s_j,t_{n+1}})$ are the average and the covariance matrix of the estimation before/after the transition, respectively.

Equations (2.19) and (2.24) can be summarized as follows.

$$\boldsymbol{X}_{j,t_{n+1}} = \boldsymbol{F}\boldsymbol{X}_{j,t_n} + \Delta t \cdot \boldsymbol{W}_{j,t_n}. \tag{2.27}$$

Here,

$$\boldsymbol{F} = \begin{bmatrix} \boldsymbol{F}_X & \boldsymbol{0} \\ \boldsymbol{0} & \boldsymbol{I}_S \end{bmatrix}, \boldsymbol{X}_{j,t_n} = \begin{bmatrix} \boldsymbol{X}_{x_j,t_n} \\ \dot{\boldsymbol{X}}_{x_j,t_n} \\ \boldsymbol{X}_{s_j,t_n} \end{bmatrix}, \boldsymbol{W}_{j,t_n} = \begin{bmatrix} \boldsymbol{w}_{x_j,t_n} \\ \boldsymbol{w}_{s_j,t_n} \end{bmatrix}.$$

$\boldsymbol{I}_S$ is a unit matrix having the same dimension as $\boldsymbol{S}$. The covariance matrix of $\boldsymbol{W}_{j,t_n}$ is defined as follows.

$$\boldsymbol{R} = \begin{bmatrix} \boldsymbol{R}_x & \boldsymbol{0} \\ \boldsymbol{0} & \boldsymbol{R}_s \end{bmatrix}. \tag{2.28}$$

Similarly, equations (2.22)-(2.23) and (2.25)-(2.26) can be summarized as follows.

$$\hat{\boldsymbol{X}}_{j,t_{n+1}} = \boldsymbol{F}\bar{\boldsymbol{X}}_{j,t_n}, \tag{2.29}$$

$$\boldsymbol{M}_{j,t_{n+1}} = \boldsymbol{F}\boldsymbol{P}_{j,t_n}\boldsymbol{F}' + \Delta t \cdot \boldsymbol{R}_{j,t_n}, \tag{2.30}$$

where

$$\boldsymbol{M}_{j,t_n} = \begin{bmatrix} \boldsymbol{M}_{x_j,t_n} & \boldsymbol{0} \\ \boldsymbol{0} & \boldsymbol{M}_{s_j,t_n} \end{bmatrix}, \hat{\boldsymbol{X}}_{j,t_n} = \begin{bmatrix} \hat{\boldsymbol{X}}_{x_j,t_n} \\ \hat{\dot{\boldsymbol{X}}}_{x_j,t_n} \\ \hat{\boldsymbol{X}}_{s_j,t_n} \end{bmatrix}, \bar{\boldsymbol{X}}_{j,t_n} = \begin{bmatrix} \bar{\boldsymbol{X}}_{x_j,t_n} \\ \bar{\dot{\boldsymbol{X}}}_{x_j,t_n} \\ \bar{\boldsymbol{X}}_{s_j,t_n} \end{bmatrix},$$

$$\boldsymbol{P} = \begin{bmatrix} \boldsymbol{P}_{x_j,t_n} & \boldsymbol{0} \\ \boldsymbol{0} & \boldsymbol{P}_{s_j,t_n} \end{bmatrix}.$$

Observation equations (2.17) and (2.18) can be summarized as follows.

$$\boldsymbol{Z}_{j,t_{n+1}} = \boldsymbol{H}\boldsymbol{X}_{j,t_{n+1}} + \boldsymbol{V}_{t_{n+1}}, \tag{2.31}$$

where

$$\boldsymbol{Z}_{j,t_{n+1}} = \begin{bmatrix} z_{x_j,t_{n+1}} \\ z_{s_j,t_{n+1}} \end{bmatrix}, \boldsymbol{H} = \begin{bmatrix} \boldsymbol{H}_x\boldsymbol{R}^{-1}_{\varphi_{ij},t_n} & \boldsymbol{0} & \boldsymbol{0} \\ \boldsymbol{0} & \boldsymbol{0} & \boldsymbol{H}_s \end{bmatrix}, \boldsymbol{X}_{t_{n+1}} = \begin{bmatrix} \boldsymbol{X}_{x_j,t_{n+1}} \\ \dot{\boldsymbol{X}}_{x_j,t_{n+1}} \\ \boldsymbol{X}_{s_j,t_{n+1}} \end{bmatrix}.$$

$\boldsymbol{V}_{t_{n+1}}$ is the measurement error vector. Its covariance matrix $\boldsymbol{Q}$ is as follows.

$$\boldsymbol{V} = \begin{bmatrix} \boldsymbol{Q}_x & \boldsymbol{0} \\ \boldsymbol{0} & \boldsymbol{Q}_s \end{bmatrix}. \tag{2.32}$$

Tracking Algorithm Finally, we apply the Kalman filter to integrate our non-synchronized observations.

The observation models and state transition models are described above. According to equations (2.11) and (2.12) in section 2.2.2, the new state of the target $\boldsymbol{X}_{t_{n+1}}$, $\hat{\boldsymbol{X}}_{t_{n+1}}$ can be estimated as follows by using the observation results (2.31).

$$\bar{\boldsymbol{X}}_{j,t_{n+1}} = \hat{\boldsymbol{X}}_{j,t_{n+1}} + \boldsymbol{K}_{j,t_{n+1}}\left(\boldsymbol{Z}_{j,t_{n+1}} - \boldsymbol{H}\hat{\boldsymbol{X}}_{j,t_{n+1}}\right), \tag{2.33}$$

where

$$\boldsymbol{K}_{j,t_{n+1}} = \boldsymbol{P}_{j,t_{n+1}}\boldsymbol{H}\boldsymbol{Q}^{-1}_{j,t_{n+1}}, \tag{2.34}$$

$$\boldsymbol{P}_{t_{n+1}} = \left(\boldsymbol{R}^{-1}_{j,t_{n+1}} + \boldsymbol{H}'\boldsymbol{Q}^{-1}_{j,t_{n+1}}\boldsymbol{H}\right)^{-1}. \tag{2.35}$$

According to the above equation, we can update the state vector for each observation $\boldsymbol{Z}_{t_{n+1}}$.

2.4.2. Finding New Targets

At the initial stage of tracking, the system must be able to detect a target object that has newly appeared in the scene. Here, we describe the method to determine the initial state of the target.

Since observation information is acquired asynchronously, the normal stereo matching cannot be used. Instead, a matching technique using Kalman filtering according to series information is used [Utsumi and Ohya, 2000].

First, information observed at four different times of the last M observations is selected from the unmatched observed information. Here, let us call the state vectors for the selected cameras $\boldsymbol{C}_a$, $\boldsymbol{C}_b$, $\boldsymbol{C}_c$ and $\boldsymbol{C}_d$ (each observation happens at t_a, t_b, t_c, and t_d, respectively).

The Kalman filtering model is then updated. Here, we use the zero value as the initial covariance ($\boldsymbol{P}_{j,t_1}^{-1} = \boldsymbol{0}$).

Following this procedure gives the estimated trajectory at four different times t_a, t_b, t_c and t_d (equation (2.29), where $\Delta t = t_i - t_d, i \in \{a, b, c, d\}$).

Let the set of observed values be $\{\boldsymbol{Z}_{t_a}, \ldots, \boldsymbol{Z}_{t_d}\}$ and the set of estimated human states be $\{\hat{\boldsymbol{X}}_{t_a}, \ldots, \hat{\boldsymbol{X}}_{t_d}\}$ (Figure 2.7).

The reliability of the correspondences among observed information can be evaluated by the following evaluation function f_{error}, which is defined as the sum of the Mahalanobis distances between the observed values and the projection of the estimated human state by equation (2.31).

$$f_{error} = \sum_{i \in \{a,b,c,d\}} \left(\boldsymbol{Z}_{t_i} - \boldsymbol{H}\hat{\boldsymbol{X}}_{t_i}\right)' \boldsymbol{Q}^{-1} \left(\boldsymbol{Z}_{t_i} - \boldsymbol{H}\hat{\boldsymbol{X}}_{t_i}\right). \qquad (2.36)$$

At the discovering node, f_{error} is calculated for all possible combinations of the last M observations.

If the errors are fewer than a threshold, this information becomes the feature point set belonging to the new human. The latest estimated position of the human is sent to the tracking node as the initial discovery position of the human at t_d.

If the number of considered observations M were to increase, the possible combinations among candidates would easily explode and it would become difficult for the discovering process to finish in a reasonable time. To avoid this, we would have to reduce the number of observations considered by assuming that the number of new targets simultaneously appearing in a scene is small. In the implementation described below, we use $M = 5$.

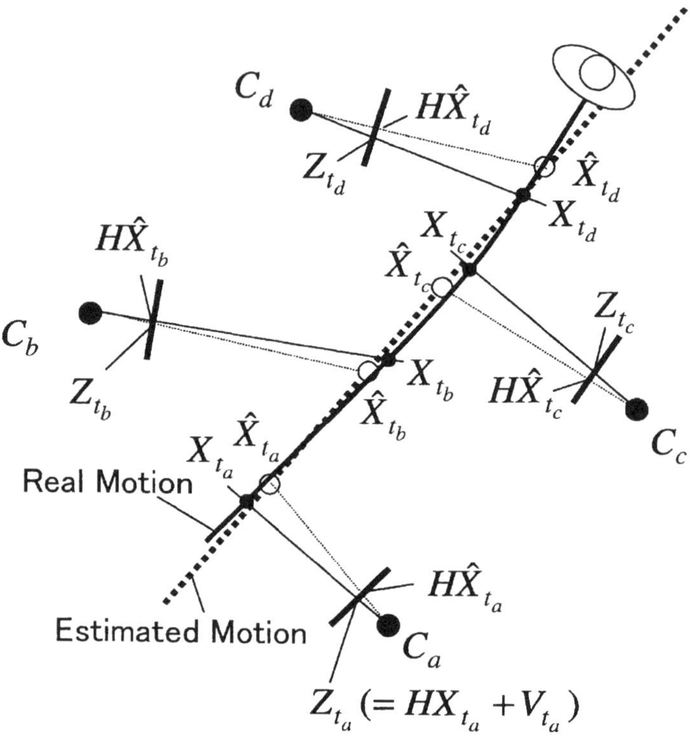

Figure 2.7. Kalman-filtering-based matching

2.5. IMPLEMENTATION

2.5.1. System Overview

In this section, we demonstrate an example of fully random observations in a human tracking task. To track human motion in an indoor scene, we have implemented a multiple-camera system using the algorithm described in the previous section. Figure 2.8 shows the configuration of the system. Here, each camera system (observation node) has its own processor, and input images are processed fully independently. At each observation node, matchings between image features and tracking targets are determined based on the estimated observation positions of the targets that are sent from the tracking node. After the matching process, the feature information corresponding to the targets is sent to the tracking node to update the tracking. The remaining (unmatched) features are sent to the discovering node.

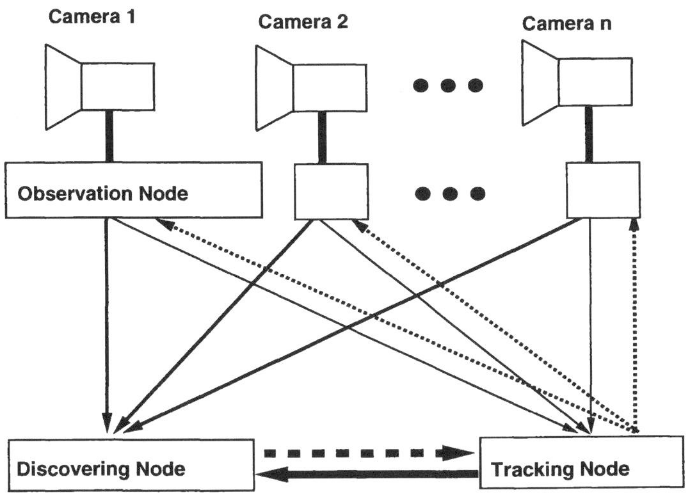

Figure 2.8. System diagram

The discovering node detects people that newly appear in the scene based on the unmatched image features sent from the observation nodes (section 2.4.2). This information is sent to the tracking node to invoke a new tracking process.

The tracking node starts and updates each tracking with the information sent by the discovering node and observation nodes (section 2.4.1).

2.5.2. Feature Extraction

This section describes the feature extraction process that takes place in each observation node.

We first perform region segmentation on the input images and then separate the images into two regions (a human region and a background region). This segmentation is based on sequential image based adaptation [Utsumi and Ohya, 1997]. In the method, information on both the target object and environment is extracted with a small amount of given knowledge about the target object. Pixel value distributions (color, intensity, etc.) for both the target object and background region are adaptively estimated from the input image sequence based on the knowledge. Then, the probability of each pixel being associated with the target object is calculated. The target region can be extracted from the calculated stochastic image (Figure 2.9). See the appendix for the details of this process.

After that, we apply distance transformation to the segmentation results. Consequently, each pixel has a certain distance from its nearest boundary pixel (Figure 2.10, top). We extract those pixels having the maximum value in the

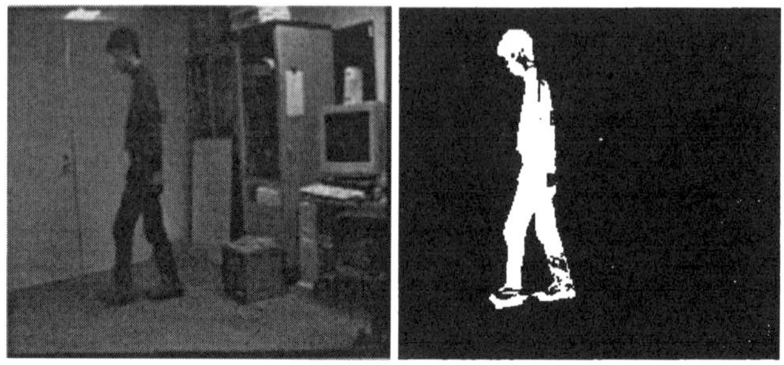

Figure 2.9. Segmentation with sequential-image-based adaptation

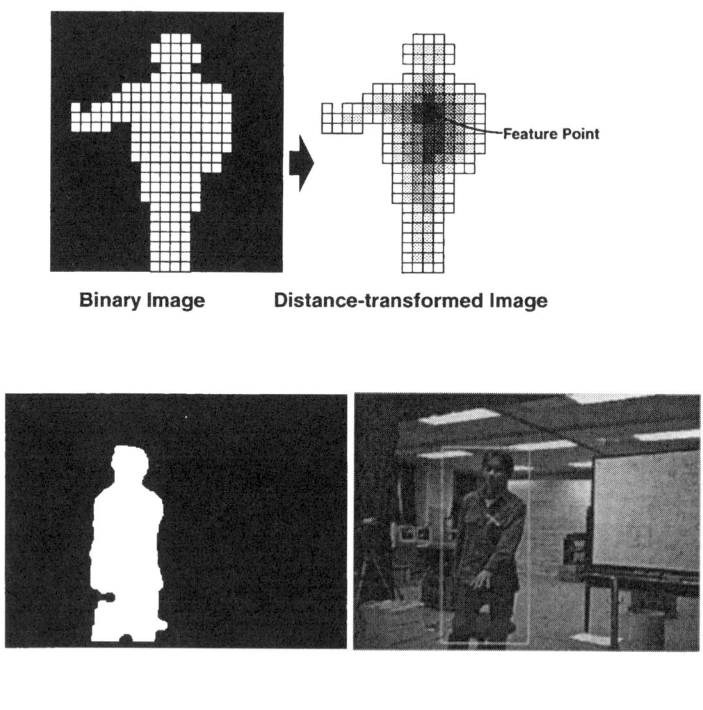

Figure 2.10. Feature extraction

transformed image as feature points (e.g., Figure 2.10, bottom). These feature points can be robustly detected regardless of arm position or body orientation [Utsumi et al., 1995; Utsumi et al., 1996].

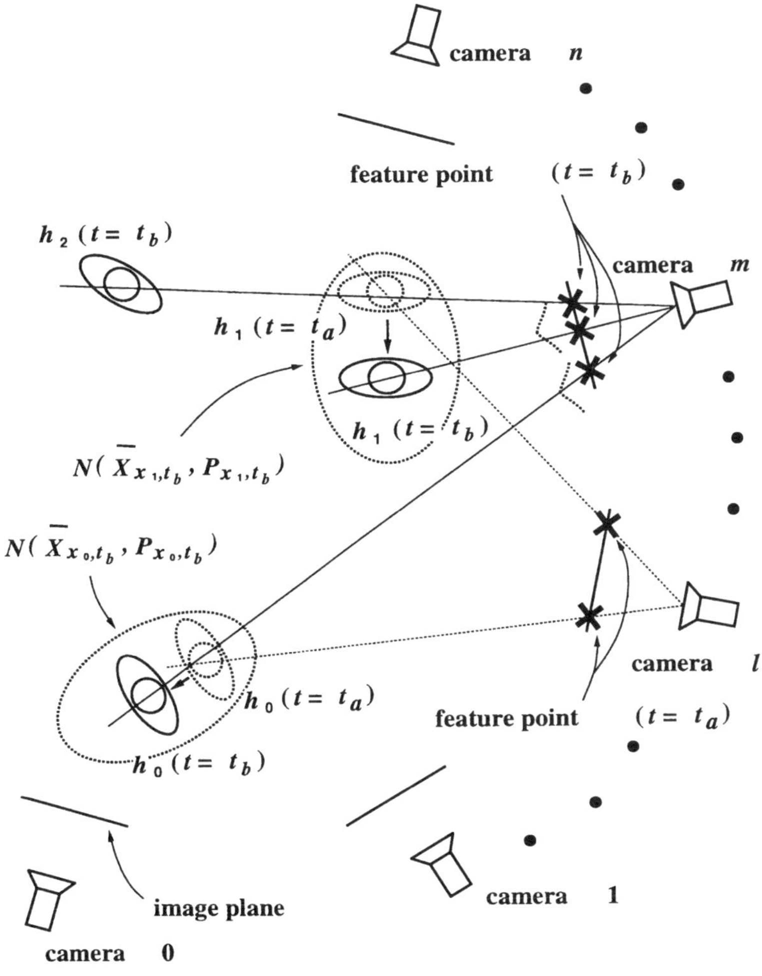

Figure 2.11. Non-synchronous observation with multiple viewpoints

2.5.3. Feature Matching at an Observation Node

Let us consider the case illustrated in Fig. 2.11. Here, we assumed that the observation for camera l took place at time t_a and the observation for camera m took place at time t_b ($t_a < t_b$). Two persons, h_0 and h_1, had already been discovered at time t_a, and person h_2 had just appeared at time t_b. In the figure, each $\times$ denotes an extracted image feature.

For h_0 and h_1, observation node m could obtain the estimated observation positions based on past observations for each from the tracking node. As the tracking model for each person is given as a Gaussian distribution (section 2.4.1, Tracking algorithm), the estimations of the observation positions are also given as Gaussian distributions (in one dimension in this case). The matching between the image features and tracking models is based on the Mahalanobis distance between them [Cox, 1993].

If some unmatched image features remain after the process, they must belong to a new object.

2.6. EXPERIMENTS

We performed the following experiments to evaluate our system.

First, we placed five observation nodes around the detection areas (Fig. 2.5). Each node had a camera and a PC (Pentium II, 400 MHz). The image processing used for the observations ran at about 5 frames/sec. One discovering node and one tracking node were connected to the PCs through a network. All of the cameras were calibrated in advance.

Figure 2.12 shows tracking results obtained for one person. Here, the broken line denotes the ground truth. The subject intended to walk along this line. As can be seen, this target was properly tracked via non-synchronous observations. Figure 2.13 shows the distribution of the time delays between succeeding observations. Here, most of the samples can be seen at around 50 ms, though the processing speed of each camera is around 5 frames/sec. This means that observations in this system are much denser than in a synchronous system.

Figure 2.14 shows a tracking result for the case of two persons. Although the two persons passed each other in the scene, the multiple-viewpoint system could track both persons properly. Figure 2.15 shows a part of the image sequences detected at each observation node.

Finally, we performed experiments using a circular motion. As already described, our algorithm assumes a straight-line motion with a constant velocity for targets, although this assumption is not often satisfied in real situations. However, we can still perform proper tracking in many cases by employing dense observations in the temporal axis. This minimizes the change in human

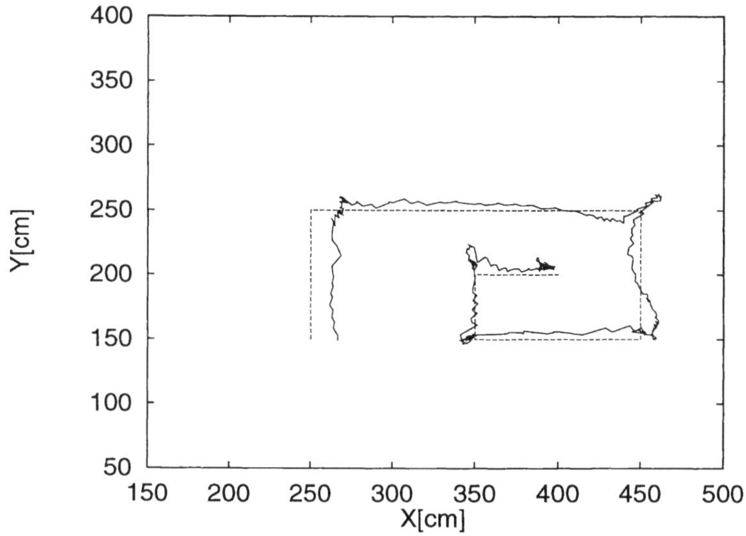

Figure 2.12. Tracking result for one person

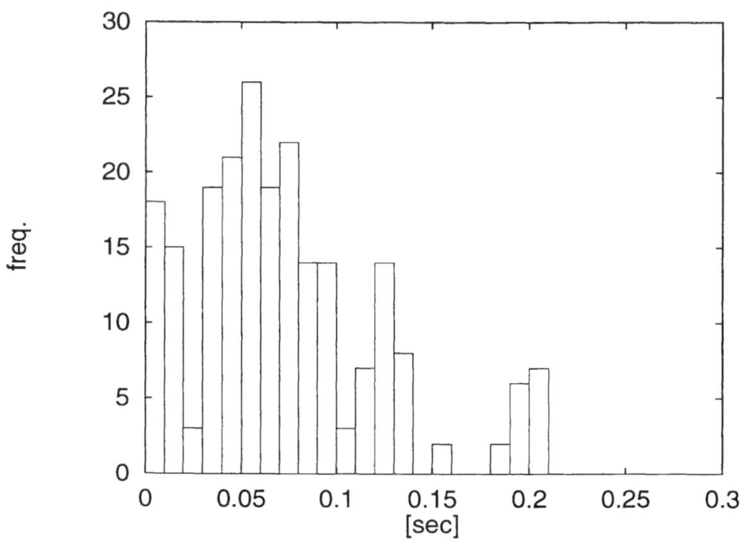

Figure 2.13. Observation intervals

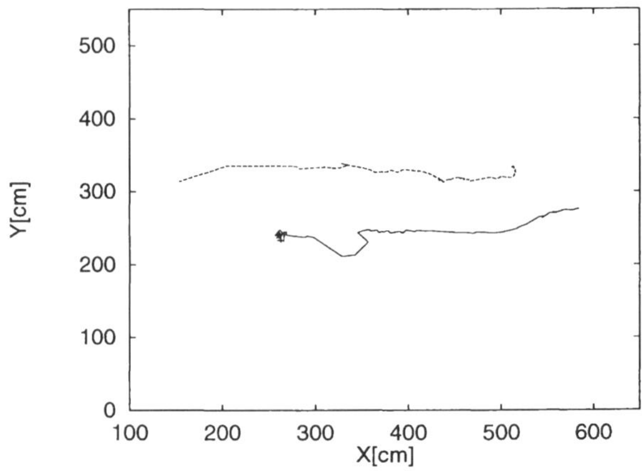

Figure 2.14. Tracking results for two persons

positions between succeeding frames, so the gap from the motion model can be considered a transition error.

We measured the tracking accuracy of our system for circular human motion by performing experiments for five subjects (subjects A – E) with six cameras. Each subject walked on a circle with a radius of 75 cm. As described above, the performance of each observation node was around 5 Hz. To examine the tracking accuracy changes due to the different performance levels of the observation nodes, we added three delays on the process at the observation nodes: 0, 0.5 and 1.0 sec.

Figure 2.16 shows the distances from the center of the circle for all subjects in the trajectories detected by the tracking process (averages and variances). (Figure 2.17 denotes the detected trajectories for one subject.) As can be seen, the detected trajectories had distances (from the center) close to 75 cm, even for the slowest case (1.0 sec delay). This indicates that our system can work effectively for a wide range of situations.

In the experiments, our system integrated observations with the Kalman filtering algorithm. The time difference of every observation was taken into account. Otherwise, the tracking would have failed due to the large gap between the target motion and the tracking model. For instance, if we had simply regarded the succeeding observations as happening simultaneously, the computation would have become much simpler. However, "No Est." (no estimation) in Figure 2.16 denotes the calculated results when we considered the succeeding five observations as happening simultaneously. As can be seen in this case, the tracking results became worse for all subjects. This means that our integration algorithm for observed information gives better results.

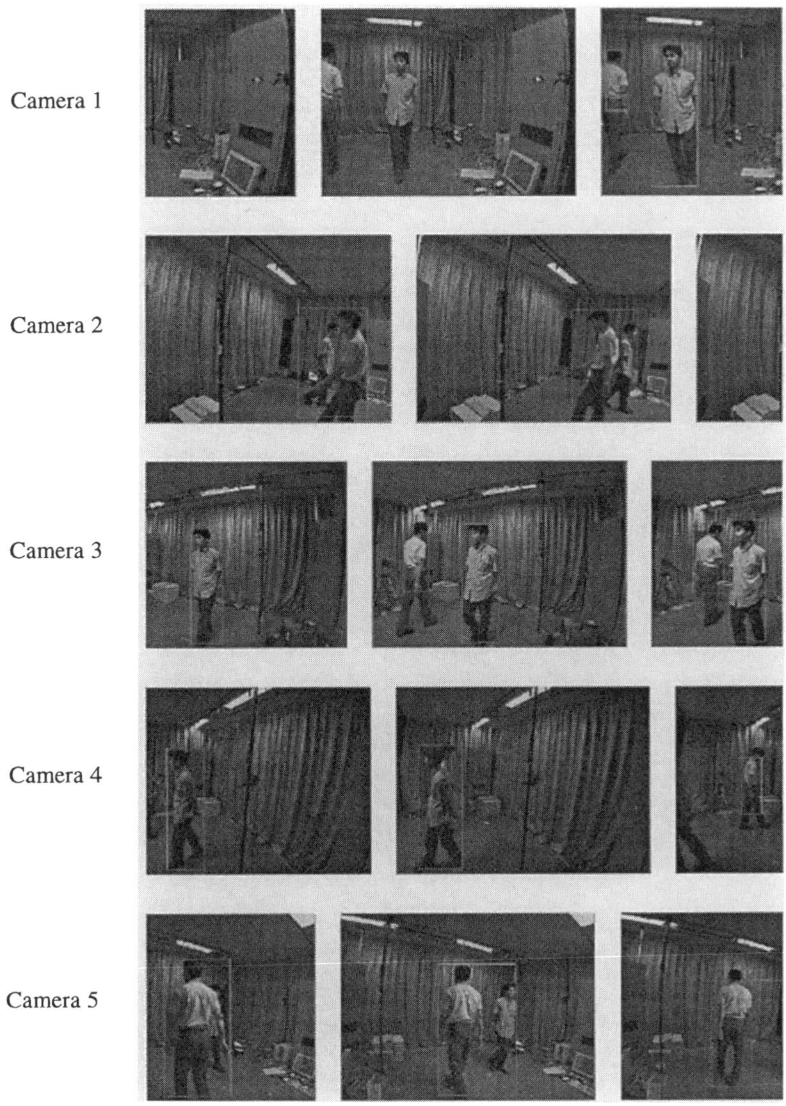

Figure 2.15. Input image sequences (two persons)

Figure 2.15 (continued).

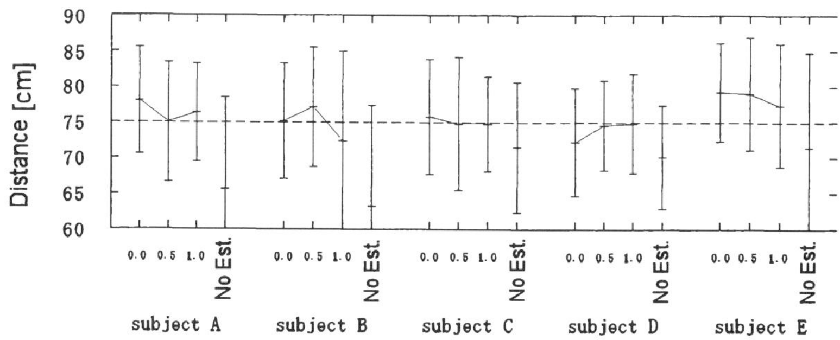

Figure 2.16. Tracking accuracy for non-linear motion (circular motion)

Furthermore, in the above experiments, tracking errors were less than 10 cm for most of the subjects for both straight and circular motions. This value is significantly smaller than the target (human body) width (of about 50–60 cm). This means that our system is accurate enough to be used for a human surveillance system, which is one of the major applications of human tracking systems.

From the above experiments, it can be seen that the proposed method can provide stable tracking of human motion by using non-synchronous observations.

In addition to position tracking, we implemented a simple motion state detection process. As mentioned above, our system tracks some additional physical properties (height, cloth color, etc.) of each person. This motion state detection is mainly based on human height observations. More specifically, if the height becomes significantly small, the system determines the state of 'sitting'. Otherwise, the state is either 'standing' or 'walking.' These two states are separated based on the target motion. The detection should be based on primitive 2-D image processing, but the current implementation simply utilizes motion vector $\dot{\boldsymbol{X}}$ to distinguish these two states. If $\dot{\boldsymbol{X}}$ is larger than a threshold value, the system determined the state as 'walking.' Figure 2.19 shows example images of these three motion states where the horizontal line shows the detected top position of the head. This position is identical to the top of the extracted silhouette.

Figure 2.18 shows motion state tracking results. As can be seen, the human motion state can be properly extracted by using human position and height information.

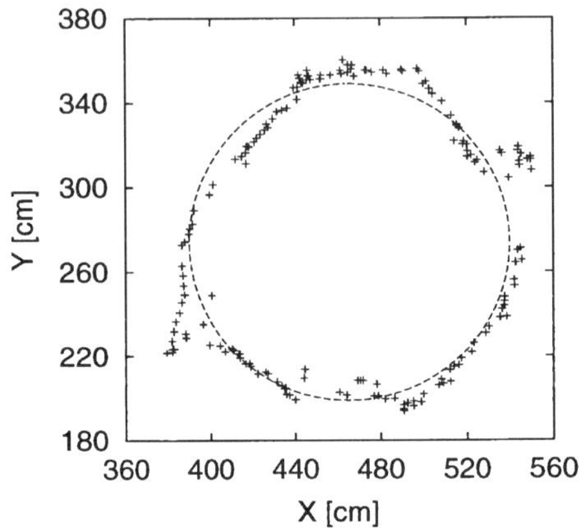

No delay

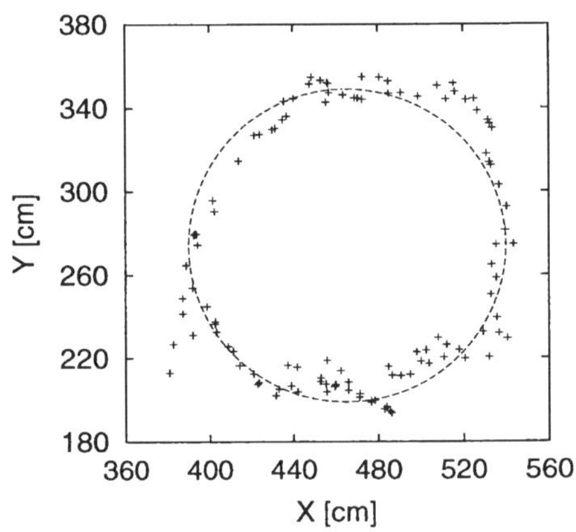

Delayed 0.5 sec

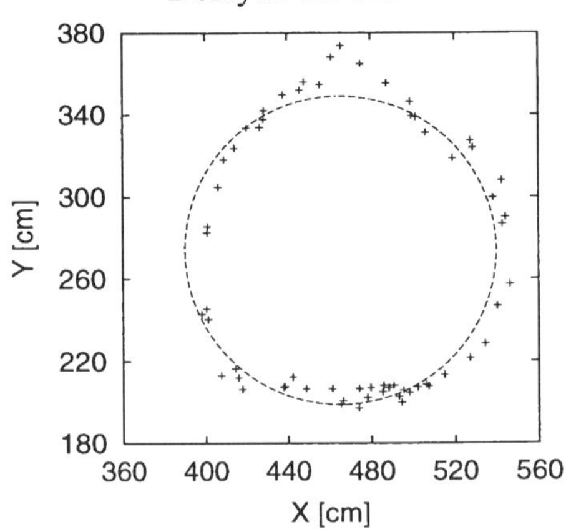

Delayed 1.0 sec

Figure 2.17. Tracking results (circular motion: subject A)

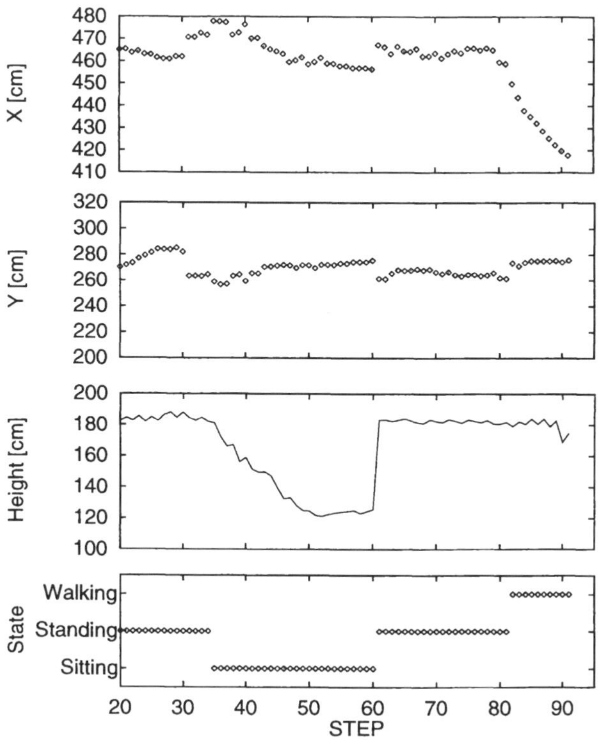

Figure 2.18. State Tracking Result (From the top: X position, Y position, human height, and detected motion state for one person's motion)

2.7. DISCUSSION AND CONCLUSIONS

In this chapter, we discussed a multiple-camera human tracking system based on non-synchronous observations. Using multiple cameras, this system tracks multiple persons in a wide area while reducing the chances of occlusion. The tracking performance is also enhanced by the multiple observations. A Kalman filter algorithm was introduced to update the tracking models for each observation. This algorithm provides less redundant observations due to the use of the multiple cameras. In addition, the algorithm simplifies the integration mechanism for multiple observations as well as the entire system configuration. This means that the system becomes robust against changes in observation conditions such as the number of cameras used and the performance differences among observation nodes. Experimental results support the superiority of this method.

On the other hand, the implementation introduced in this chapter has some limitations. In the tracking and image processing parts, we discussed the algo-

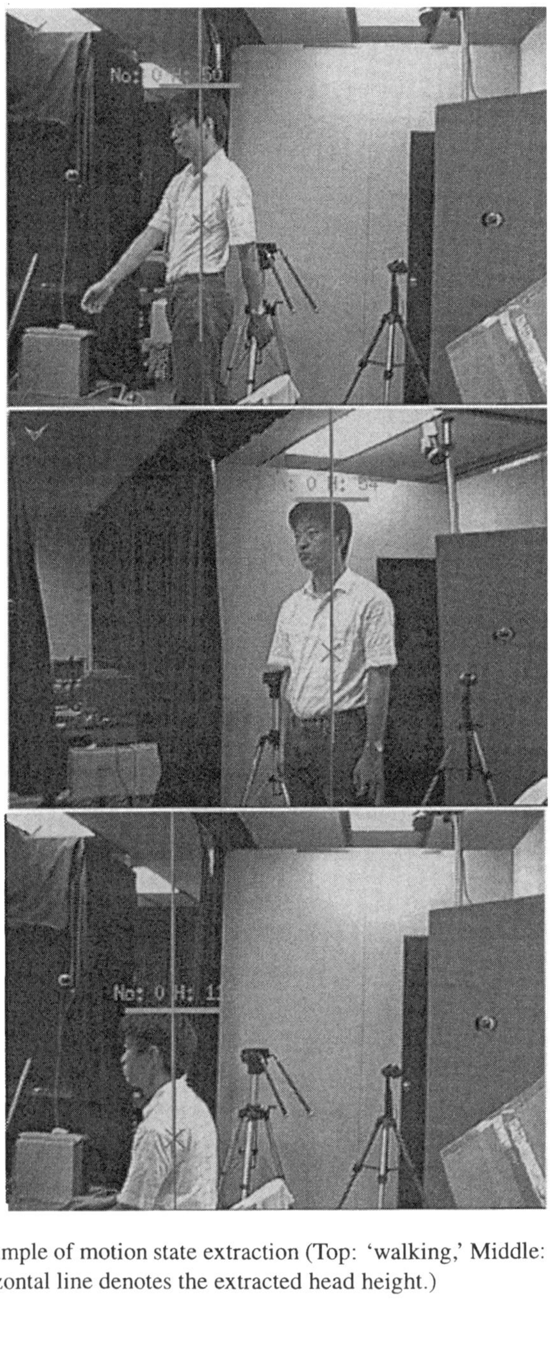

Figure 2.19. Example of motion state extraction (Top: 'walking,' Middle: 'standing,' Bottom: 'sitting.' The horizontal line denotes the extracted head height.)

rithm by using horizontal observations to simplify the explanation. All cameras are placed at a similar level (height) as the persons in the experiments. However, our algorithm for non-synchronous observations can be easily expanded to cameras used at various positions. In fact, a top-view camera can also be used [Utsumi et al., 2001].

Furthermore, our system employs a region segmentation method based on sequential images for feature extraction. Using this technique, the system can track persons even if there are gradual changes in the environment. However, this method does not work properly when a large number of changes occur, such as in an outdoor scene. We are investigating a more robust method to extract human features to overcome the challenges posed by such situations.

Appendix: Image Segmentation using Sequential-image-based Adaptation

Here, we describe our segmentation algorithm using sequential image based adaptation. Raw images have too much information, and therefore, direct model matching with a raw image requires both a huge model construction cost and a large computational cost for the reconstruction. A segmented image based approach is advantageous in reducing these costs.

However, conventional segmentation algorithms often produce unstable results. Most of the popular algorithms (e.g., thresholding, background subtraction, etc.) assume a static environment, so they no longer work properly once the environment is changed. To overcome instabilities, we have to make the system more adaptive to environmental changes.

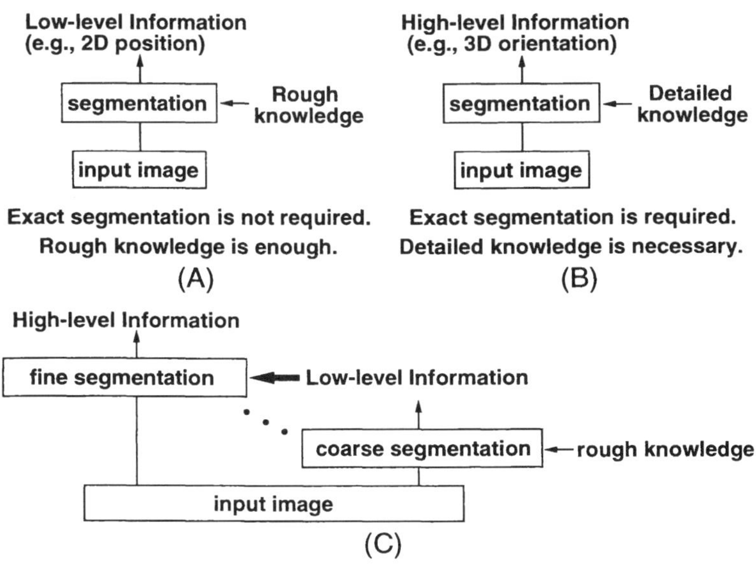

Figure 2.A.1. Hierarchical Adaptation

Fortunately, the degree of instability is not the same for all levels of information. For instance, in human tracking, approximate positions (we call them low-level information here) can be determined even if the segmentation is not perfect. This means that the assumptions (knowledge) to obtain such low-level information can be rough (Figure 2.A.1(A)). Conversely, to extract a person's orientation, face position, hand motion, etc. (i.e., high-level information), fine segmentation is necessary. In this case, detailed knowledge about the target (intensity, color, texture) is required to accomplish the detection (Figure 2.A.1(B)).

Our idea is to integrate these different levels of information and achieve fine segmentation using an information hierarchy. First, we do coarse segmentation using inter-frame subtraction and our rough knowledge about the target confirms the segmentation result. Then, we refine the segmentation criteria at every frame using the extracted low-level information and receive fine segmentation results (Figure 2.A.1 (C)). After that, high level information detection (i.e., human posture estimation) is performed.

Next, we give the basic algorithm to perform the adaptive segmentation.

Segmentation Algorithm

Let us consider the situation in which a target region (e.g., a human region) T is moving around in a sequence of images (Figure 2.A.2). $P(T)$ is the mean size ratio of the target in an image. We assume that the target object visits positions in the images in a uniform manner in the long sequence. The target object can be observed at every pixel with a probability $P(T)$. $P_l(v)$ is the probability that pixel value v is observed at a pixel l ($l \in \Omega$, Ω is the set of all pixels in an image). When we assume that the distribution of $P_l(v)$ is equal for all pixels, we simply denote the global distribution with $P(v)$.

We also define global distributions $P(v|T)$ for the target region and $P(v|B)$ for the background region. (The local distribution for the background region is $P_l(v|B)$. We consider that the distribution for the target region is equal everywhere in an image here.) These distributions have the following relations.

$$P(v) = P(T)P(v|T) + (1 - P(T))P(v|B). \quad (2.A.1)$$

$$P_l(v) = P(T)P(v|T) + (1 - P(T))P_l(v|B). \quad (2.A.2)$$

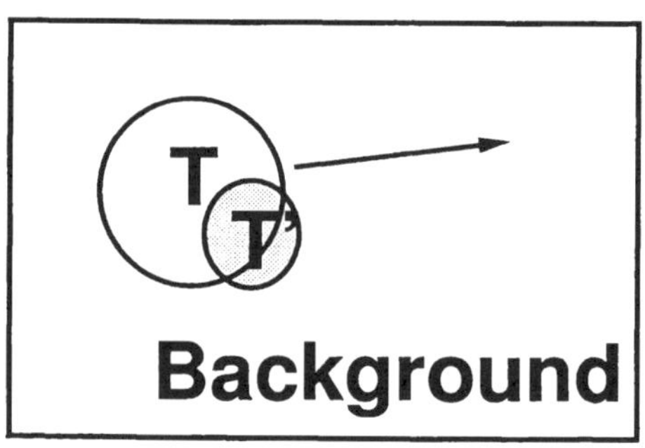

Figure 2.A.2. Coarse Segmentation

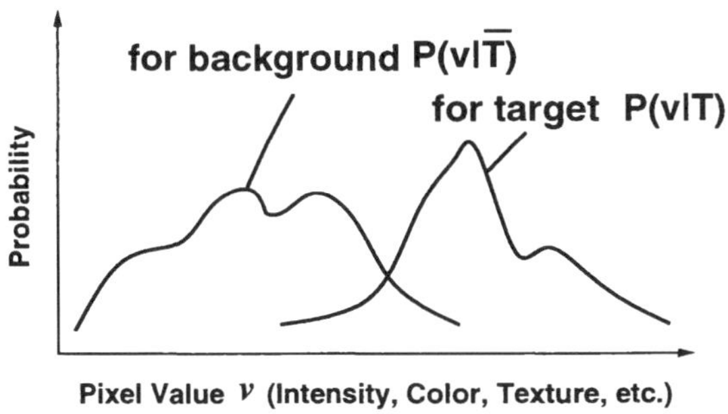

Figure 2.A.3. Pixel Value Distributions

If distributions $P(v|T)$ and $P(v|B)$ are given, the probability $P(T|v)$ that a pixel having the value v belongs to the target can be calculated as follows by using the Bayes rule.

$$\begin{aligned} P(T|v) &= \frac{P(T)P(v|T)}{P(v)} \\ &= \frac{P(T)P(v|T)}{P(T)P(v|T) + (1 - P(T))P(v|B)}. \end{aligned} \tag{2.A.3}$$

Using the local distributions,

$$P_l(T|v) = \frac{P(T)P(v|T)}{P_l(v)}. \tag{2.A.4}$$

Using the above equations, we can translate an input image to a stochastic image, where each pixel has the probability of belonging to the target object. This process can be considered as a kind of segmentation. (Indeed, the translated image can be easily binarized by simple thresholding.)

However, in real situations, it is difficult to know about $P(v|T)$ and $P(v|B)$ in advance. Here, we consider estimating these distributions from a sequence of input images.

Now, let us assume that we can select a region T' that includes a part of the target region T in the input images using a priori knowledge about the target object (Figure 2.A.2). $P_t(v|T')$ is the pixel value distribution of all observed pixels included in T' until time t. Assuming that each pixel in T can be selected into T' with equivalent probability, $P_t(v|T')$ converges as follows.

$$\lim_{t\to\infty} P_t(v|T') = P(v|T') = kP(v|T) + (1-k)P(v|B). \tag{2.A.5}$$

(k is the ratio of pixels in $T \cap T'$ to T'.)

In addition, $P_t(v)$, the frequency distribution of all of the observed pixel values until time t converges to $P(v)$ is as follows.

$$\lim_{t\to\infty} P_t(v) = P(v). \tag{2.A.6}$$

Considering local distributions, the above equations can be rewritten as follows.

$$\lim_{t\to\infty} P_{l,t}(v|T') = P_l(v|T') = kP_l(v|T) + (1-k)P_l(v|B). \tag{2.A.7}$$

$$\lim_{t\to\infty} P_{l,t}(v) = P_l(v). \tag{2.A.8}$$

We use the above $P_t(v|T')$ and $P_t(v)$ to approximately calculate equation (2.A.3).

$$\begin{aligned}\hat{P}(T|v) &= \lim_{t\to\infty} \frac{P(T)P_t(v|T')}{P_t(v)} = \frac{P(T)P(v|T')}{P(v)} \\ &= \frac{P(T)P(v|T)}{P(v)} + (1-k)\boldsymbol{R}(v). \end{aligned} \tag{2.A.9}$$

Here,

$$\boldsymbol{R}(v) = \frac{P(T)}{P(v)} \left(P(v|\bar{T}) - P(v|T)\right). \tag{2.A.10}$$

In the result of (2.A.9), the second term $\boldsymbol{R}(v)$ denotes the estimation error caused by the inclusion of the background region into T'. If $k = 1$ (i.e., all of the pixels in T' belong to T), the result becomes identical to equation (2.A.3). We can expect the best performance in this case. In contrast, according to the decrease of k, the error in equation (2.A.3) increases. When the selection of T' becomes full at random, the ratio k becomes $P(T)$. In this case, $\hat{P}(T|v)$ becomes a constant value for all v.

$$\hat{P}(T|v) = P(T). \tag{2.A.11}$$

This means segmentation is impossible.

Even in this case, however, segmentation is still possible to some extent if the local distributions $P_l(v)$ are known. Using the local distributions, equation (2.A.9) becomes

$$\hat{P}_l(T|v) = \frac{P(T)P(v|T)}{P_l(v)} \tag{2.A.12}$$

$$= P(T)\frac{P(T)P(v|T) + (1-P(T))P(v|B)}{P(T)P(v|T) + (1-P(T))P_l(v|B)}. \tag{2.A.13}$$

The result of the equation becomes large when $P_l(v|B)$ becomes small (i.e., the input value differs from the background value). This can be considered as a kind of background subtraction.

As mentioned above, our algorithm works adaptively for an input image sequence and produces a stochastic image regarding the target's presence. In the next section, we implement this algorithm in some definite image features.

Implementation

We employ image subtraction among succeeding frames to extract primitive target regions (i.e., coarse segmentation). Our system has a model (knowledge) that considers the target size and motion. When an extracted result matches this model, the corresponding region is determined to be the target region T'.

Figure 2.A.4 shows the extraction process. Let $V_t = \{v_{l,t}|l \in \Omega\}$ be an input image at time t. Then, $S_{i,j} = \{s^l_{i,j}|l \in \Omega\}$, the subtraction image between V_i and V_j, can be produced as follows.

$$s^l_{i,j} = \begin{cases} 0 & (\text{when} |v_{l,i} - v_{l,j}| \leq threshold,) \\ 1 & (\text{else}). \end{cases} \tag{2.A.14}$$

We generate mask image $M_t = \{m_{l,t}|l \in \Omega\}$ by overlapping several frames of subtracted images.

$$M_t = \left(\bigcap_{i=t-m}^{t-1} S_{i,t}\right) \bigcap \left(\bigcap_{i=t+1}^{t+n} S_{t,i}\right). \tag{2.A.15}$$

Pixel value distributions are updated only when the size of the mask image is in a certain range.

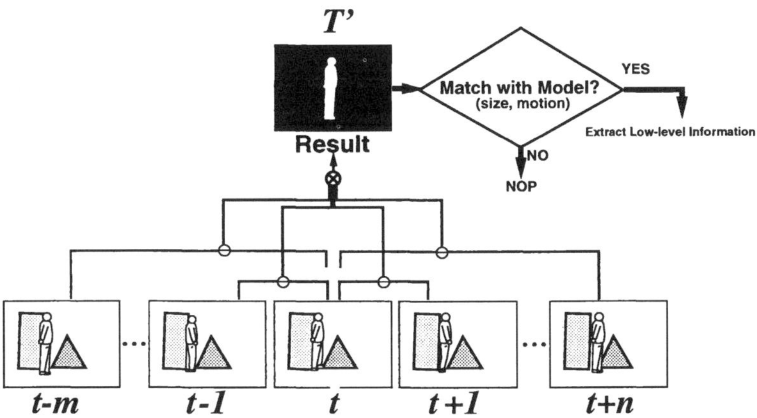

Figure 2.A.4. Detecting Low-level Information

Experiments

Here, we show experimental results using monochrome images as an example. Let $Y_t = \{y_{l,t}|l \in \Omega\}$ be an input intensity image at time t. In the case, equation (2.A.12) can be rewritten as follows.

$$\hat{P}_l(T|y) = \frac{P(T)P(y|T)}{P_l(y)}. \tag{2.A.16}$$

We estimate $P(y|T)$ and $P_l(y)$ as follows. To simplify the problem, we assume that the distribution $P_l(y)$ is a beta distribution, and estimate its averages and variances as follows.

We increment both average image $\overline{Y}_t = \{\overline{y}_{l,t}|l \in \Omega\}$ and square average image $\overline{Y^2}_t = \left\{\overline{y^2}_{l,t}|l \in \Omega\right\}$.

$$\overline{y}_{l,t} = \rho y_{l,t} + (1-\rho)\overline{y}_{t-1}. \tag{2.A.17}$$

$$\overline{y^2}_{l,t} = \rho y_{l,t}^2 + (1-\rho)\overline{y^2}_{t-1}. \tag{2.A.18}$$

Here, $0 < \rho << 1$. Then, we calculate the parameters of the beta distribution for each pixel as follows.

$$\alpha(\overline{y}, \overline{y^2}) = \frac{\overline{y}(\overline{y} - \overline{y^2})}{\overline{y^2} - \overline{y}^2}, \beta(\overline{y}, \overline{y^2}) = \frac{\overline{y^2}\,\overline{y} - \overline{y}^2 - \overline{y^2}}{\overline{y^2} - \overline{y}^2}. \tag{2.A.19}$$

$$P_{l,t}(y) = f_{\alpha(\overline{y}_{l,t}, \overline{y^2}_{l,t}), \beta(\overline{y}_{l,t}, \overline{y^2}_{l,t})}(y). \tag{2.A.20}$$

Here, $f_{\alpha,\beta}$ denotes a beta distribution function with parameters α and β. In addition, we increment histogram $P_t(y|T)$.

$$N_t = \sum_{l \in \Omega} m_{l,t} \tag{2.A.21}$$

Here, $m_{l,t} = 1$ only when pixel l is included in the coarse segmented region.
For each y,

$$n_{y,t} = \sum_{\{l|y_l = y\}} m_l. \tag{2.A.22}$$

$$P_t(y|T) = \rho\frac{n_{y,t}}{N_t} + (1-\rho)P_{t-1}(y|T). \tag{2.A.23}$$

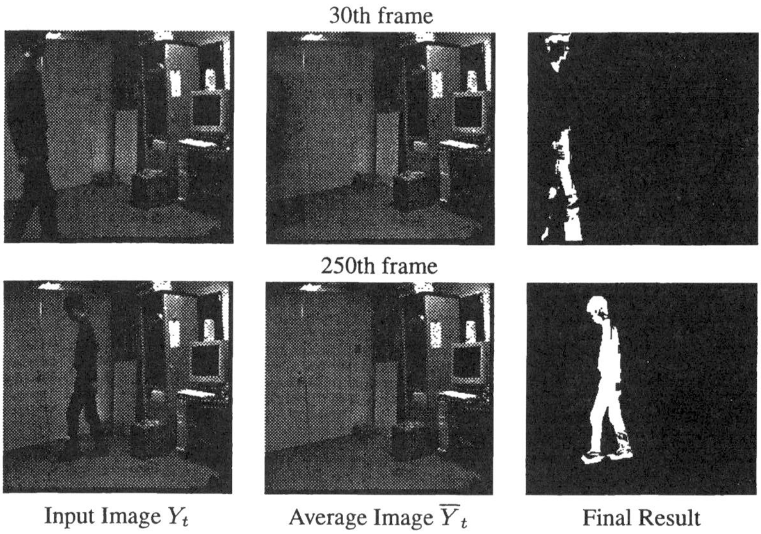

Figure 2.A.5. Segmentation using Intensity Information

From equations (2.A.16), (2.A.20) and (2.A.23), stochastic image $Z_t = \left\{\hat{P}_{l,t}(T|y_{l,t})|l \in \Omega\right\}$ can be produced.

Figure 2.A.5 shows the segmentation results. In this case, a human moved around in an image sequence. The top images show results taken at the 30th frame. The bottom images are at the 250th frame.

Figure 2.A.6 shows results for another image sequence. In this case, a hand moved in the scene. The top images show results taken at the 500th frame. Though we changed the background after the 500th frame, the pixel value distribution was improved and the segmentation became stable again (bottom images).

As can be seen, renovation of the pixel value distribution greatly improves the stability of the segmentation.

Notes

1. Strictly speaking, we need to derive the algorithm with a framework of minimum mean square estimation. However, equivalent results are obtained when we assume Gaussian distributions for the system.

References

Azarbayejani, A. and Pentland, A. (1996). Real-time self-calibrating stereo person tracking using 3-d shape estimation from blob features. In *Proceedings of 13th International Conference on Pattern Recognition*, pages 627–632.

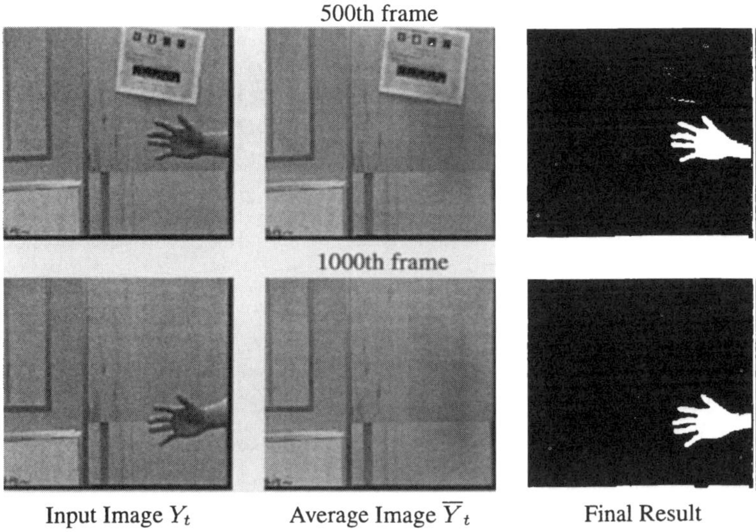

Figure 2.A.6. Segmentation using Intensity Information

Cai, Q. and Aggarwal, J. K. (1996). Tracking human motion using multiple cameras. In *Proceedings of 13th International Conference on Pattern Recognition*, pages 68–72.

Cox, I. J. (1993). A review of statical data association techniques for motion correspondence. *International Journal of Computer Vision*, 10:1:53–66.

Gavrila, D. M. and Davis, L. S. (1996). 3-d model-based tracking of humans in action: a multi-view approach. In *Proc. of Computer Vision and Pattern Recognition*, pages 73–80.

Johnson, M. P., Maes, P., and Darrell, T. (1994). Evolving visual routines. In *Proc. of Artificial Life IV*, pages 198–209.

Kalman, R. E. (1960). A new approach to linear filtering and prediction problems. *Trans. ASME, J. Basic Eng.*, 82D(1):34–45.

Khan, S. and Shah, M. (2000). Tracking people in presence of occlusion. In *Proceedings of 4th Asian Conference on Computer Vision*, pages 1132–1137.

Matthies, L. and Shafer, S. A. (1987). Error modeling in stereo navigation. *IEEE Robotics and Automation*, RA-3(3):239–248.

Nakazawa, A., Kato, H., and Inokuchi, S. (1998). Human tracking using distributed vision systems. In *Proc. of 14th International Conference on Pattern Recognition*, pages 593–596.

O'Rourke, J. and Badler, N. J. (1980). Model-based image analysis of human motion using constraint propagation. *IEEE Pattern Analysis and Machine Intelligence*, 2(6):522–536.

Rohr, K. (1994). Towards model-based recognition of human movements in image sequences. *CVGIP: Image Understanding*, 59(1):94–115.

Segen, J. and Pingali, S. (1996). A camera-based system for tracking people in real time. In *Proceedings of 13th International Conference on Pattern Recognition*, pages 63–67.

Utsumi, A., Miyasato, T., Kishino, F., and Nakatsu, R. (1995). Real-time hand gesture recognition system. In *Proc. of 2nd Asian Conference on Computer Vision*, volume II, pages 667–671.

Utsumi, A., Miyasato, T., Kishino, F., and Nakatsu, R. (1996). Hand gesture recognition system using multiple cameras. In *13th International Conference on Pattern Recognition*, pages 219–224.

Utsumi, A., Mori, H., Ohya, J., and Yachida, M. (1998). Multiple-view-based tracking of multiple humans. In *Proc. of 14th International Conference on Pattern Recognition*, pages 597–601.

Utsumi, A. and Ohya, J. (1997). Hand image segmentation using sequential-image-based hierarchical adaptation. In *International Conference on Image Processing*, pages 208–211.

Utsumi, A. and Ohya, J. (2000). Multiple-camera-based human tracking using non-synchronous observations. In *Proceedings of Fourth Asian Conference on Computer Vision*, pages 1034–1039.

Utsumi, A., Yang, H., and Tetsutani, N. (2001). Vision-based human tracking using a top-view approach with non-synchronous multiple observations. In *Proceedings of International Workshop on Advanced Image Technology*, pages 193–198.

Wren, C., Azarbayejani, A., Darrell, T., and Pentland, A. (1996). Pfinder: Real-time tracking of the human body. In *SPIE proceeding vol. 2615*, pages 89–98.

Yamamoto, M. and Koshikawa, K. (1991). Human motion analysis based on a robot arm model. In *Proc. of Computer Vision and Pattern Recognition*, pages 664–665.

Yi, J.-W. and Oh, J.-H. (1997). Recursive resolving algorithm for multiple stereo and motion matches. *Image and Vision Computing*, 15:181–196.

Chapter 3

POSTURE ESTIMATION

Jun Ohya
Waseda University
Global Information and Telecommunication Institute
Bldg. 29-7, 1-3-10 Nishi-Waseda, Shinjuku-ku, Tokyo 169-0051, Japan

Abstract This chapter describes our real-time methods for locating significant points on the human body to determine posture. The three systems we created are presented in the order in which they were developed, where the second and third were based on the first and second, respectively. The first system heuristically locates significant points on the body by analyzing the contour of the human silhouette extracted from the background in a monocular image. The positions of the elbows and knees, which are in general difficult to locate by the contour analysis, are estimated using a learning procedure based on a genetic algorithm. To enable posture estimation in 3D, the second system uses three cameras that observe the person from three directions. However, the second system still uses empirical knowledge about human bodies and heuristic rules; therefore, postures that can be estimated by the second system were limited. For the third system, a function based contour curvature analysis method, which does not need any empirical knowledge nor heuristic rules, was developed. To cope with self-occlusions, image difference in local areas is also utilized. The posture estimation methods are successfully applied to an application in virtual environments, where the estimated postures are reproduced in avatars (computer graphics characters) in real-time.

Keywords: Posture estimation, human silhouette analysis, contour analysis, 3D reconstruction, tracking, occlusion, image difference

3.1. Introduction

Humans can assume a variety of postures by moving their body parts such as arms, hands, legs and head; more specifically, by rotating articulations and/or bending/stretching the spine. The goal of posture estimation methods is to estimate parameters that specify postures. Then, what should be appropriate posture parameters? In theory, the posture of a human is specified in terms of angle values for each degree of freedom of each rotational articulation as well as the orientation and curvature of the spine. Ideally, the posture estimation method should be able to estimate these parameters, but in general, direct estimation is difficult for computer vision based methods. Another reasonable representation of postures is to specify the 3D positions of some significant points on the surface of the human body such as the extremities and the top of the head. Given the 3D positions of the significant points, angle values of articulations and the spine's parameters could be calculated or approximated by a method such as inverse-kinematics. This chapter deals with methods for estimating the positions of the significant points.

Approaches to measure or estimate postures are classified roughly into two categories: contact and non-contact type. A magnetic sensor, like a Polhemus, is a typical example of a contact type device; it is easy to use and the acquired data is quite accurate, but it is cumbersome and hard to handle since it has to be worn by a person at all the time. This limits the use of contact type systems in various applications. In contrast, non-contact type image analysis methods reduce the burden imposed on users.

In image analysis methods, human posture description from a still scene has been studied [Pentland 1990; Pentland et al., 1991a; Terzopoulos et al., 1991; Kameda et al., 1993]. Here, human images are segmented into parts, and each part is fitted by deformable models [Pentland 1990; Pentland et al., 1991b]; unfortunately, this strategy requires range images, which cannot easily be acquired in many realistic applications. Similarly, superquadrics have been fitted to 2-D human doll images [Terzopoulos et al., 1991]. For this, some reference points on the human are given manually. Human body part models have been matched to a monocular human silhouette image [Kameda et al., 1993]; the contour based matching used in this method is sensitive to image noise, and accurate parameter estimation for arbitrary postures is a difficult task for monocular image analysis. Human motion in a monocular image sequence has been analyzed in a model-based manner using constraints and knowledge of human motion [Pentland et al., 1991b; Chen et al., 1992; Kurakake et al., 1992; Rohr 1993; Yamamoto et al., 2000]. Although these methods can deal with 3-D human movements, they are not easily applied to arbitrary human postures, because they require constraints and knowledge. Moreover, in some of these methods, manual fitting of a human model to some frames is used. The methods proposed in [Ohya et al., 1994; Gavrila et al., 1996] can also deal with 3-D postures, but body models and large computation cost are required, and their processing rate is particularly suited for off-line jobs.

In contrast, there are only a few methods which work in real-time. Pfinder [Wren et al., 1996; Azarbayejani et al., 1996], one of the real-time methods, tracks the head, hands, and feet based on models from a contour and color information of the body, and it predicts model parameters using a Kalman filter. However, it still has the following problems: less freedom of movement and sensitivity to environmental factors such as the appearance of the background, lightings, and clothing. The W4 system [Haritaoglu et al., 1998] is another promising real-time system, which was developed to track human movements in 3D [Horprasert et al., 1998]. If cardboard model fitting to each body part and template matchig of salient body parts in the color images work stably, good performance is expected from this system. To cope with arbitrary postures, the current W4's tracking system based on dynamics/kinematics model of the human body and the Kalman filter might need some additional reinforcement.

This chapter describes our real-time methods for locating significant points on a human body. The three systems described here were developed sequentially: the second and third were developed based on the first and second, respectively. The first system [Iwasawa et al., 1997] heuristically locates significant points by analyzing the contour of the human silhouette extracted from the background in a monocular image. The positions of the elbows and knees, which are in general difficult to locate by the contour analysis method, are estimated using a learning procedure based on a genetic algorithm. Since the posture estimation results are only in 2D, three cameras observe the person from three directions so that the second system can estimate postures in 3D. However, the second system [Iwasawa et al., 2000] still uses heuristic rules and empirical knowledge about the human body, and thus can estimate only a limited range of postures. For the third system [Takahashi et al., 2000], a function based contour analysis method, which does not need any empirical knowledge or heuristic rules, was developed. To cope with self-occlusions, image difference in local areas is also utilized. After observing and processing the initial calibration pose, the third system keeps estimating postures of the person in 3D in real-time.

This chapter is organized as follows. Sections 3.2, 3.3, and 3.4 describe the heuristic method for estimating postures in 2D (the first system), the heuristic method for estimating postures in 3D (the second system) , and the non-heuristic method for estimating postures in 3D (the third system). As an application of the posture estimation methods described here, the real-time systems in which the estimated postures are reproduced in avatars (computer graphics characters) in virtual environments are introduced in Section 3.5. Summary of the three systems and their remaining issues are described in Section 3.6.

3.2. A Heuristic Method for Estimating Postures in 2D

3.2.1. Outline

A person whose posture is to be estimated is observed by an infrared camera that can acquire thermal images at a video rate. For each frame, significant features, such as the top of the head, are heuristically located in the thermal image according to the following image processing based procedures.

1 The silhouette, which corresponds to body area in the thermal image, is extracted by thresholding the thermal image, and then the center of gravity is obtained from a distance-transformed thermal image.

2 The orientation of the upper half of the body (above the waist) is obtained based on the orientation in the previous frame.

3 Significant points, namely the tips of the hands and feet, and the top of the head, are located by a heuristic contour analysis of the human silhouette.

These processes are detailed in Section 3.2.2. Note that the method in this section uses an infrared camera so as to facilitate the extraction of the human silhoutte at each frame. However, as described in Sections 3.3 and 3.4, non-infrared color CCD cameras can be used instead, as long as the silhouettes can be extracted from the background based on color alone.

Before the processing of the image frames for the computation of the pose parameters, the initial frame needs to be calibrated. During the calibration, the person needs to keep the posture shown in Fig. 3.1, standing upright and keeping both arms horizontal. The significant points are located in the silhouette image for the calibration pose. The height of the circumscribed rectangle of the human body silhouette and distances between the center of gravity of the body and significant points are stored as a reference.

After the above processes in each frame, main joint positions are estimated based on the located positions of the significant points using a genetic algorithm (GA) based learning procedure, which is explained in Section 3.2.3.

3.2.2. Locating significant points of the human body

3.2.2.1 Center of Gravity of the Human Body. An infrared CCD camera measures electro magnetic radiation emitted by objects in a scene and acquires thermal images whose pixel values show temperature. Since the temperatures of human body and background are generally different, a simple thresholding can extract the human silhouette (the area corresponding to the body) from the background regardless of lighting conditions and colors of the clothes the person wears and the environment. An example of a thermal image

Figure 3.1. Posture used for the calibration

Figure 3.2. Example of a thermal image (gray-levels represent temperature values)

is shown in Fig. 3.2, where gray-levels represent temperature values (dark and light levels are low and high temperature values, respectively). Let f_{ij} denote the thresholded (binary) thermal image, where i and j are the vertical and horizontal coordinates of the image, respectively. Here $f_{ij} = 1$ for regions within the silhouette, and 0 for the background. After this, the remaining processes are applied only to human body region which has largest area in f_{ij}.

To obtain the center of gravity (CoG) of the body accurately regardless of the pose of the arms and the legs, a distance transformation is applied to f_{ij}, (specifically, to the pixels whose values are 1). Each pixel of the distance-transformed image d_{ij} (Fig. 3.3) has values representing the distance between the pixel and the nearest contour pixel (bright intensities and dark intensities indicate large and small distance values, respectively), where $d_{ij} = 0$ for pixels with $f_{ij} = 0$. The coordinates (I_c, J_c) of CoG are calculated by the following equations:

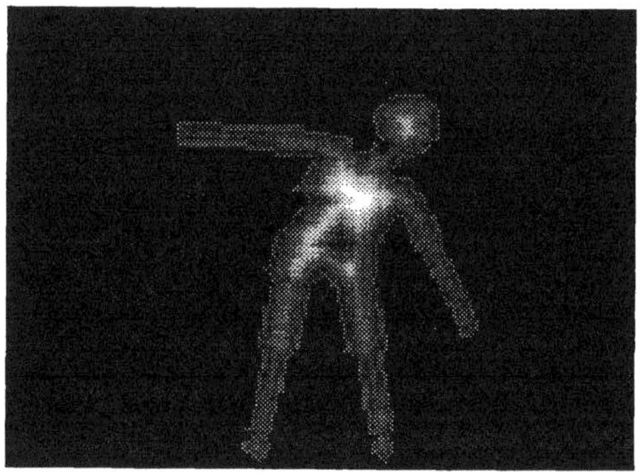

Figure 3.3. Distance-transformed image with a silhouette contour (gray-levels represent distance values: bright and dark levels indicate large and small values, respectively)

$$I_c = \frac{\mathrm{M}(1, 0)}{\mathrm{M}(0, 0)} \tag{3.1}$$

$$J_c = \frac{\mathrm{M}(0, 1)}{\mathrm{M}(0, 0)} \tag{3.2}$$

where

$$\mathrm{M}(p, q) = \sum_i \sum_j i^p j^q d_{ij}. \tag{3.3}$$

As indicated in Eqs. (3.1) and (3.2), the coordinates I_c and J_c are weighted with the distances, which take small values in narrow areas such as arms and legs and large values around CoG. This means influences by the arms and legs can be suppressed by Eqs. (3.1) and (3.2). CoG is used as the reference point for the human body in the subsequent processes described in the following sections.

3.2.2.2 Orientation of the Upper Half of the Human Body. The orientation of the upper half of the body is needed for the subsequent processes. A candidate for the orientation is the principal axis of inertia of the human silhouette, but the calculation of the principal axis is highly sensitive to changes in the pose of the arms. Therefore, to suppress the contribution of the arms in the distance-transformed image d_{ij}, a Gaussian distribution whose symmetrical axis is fitted to the orientation angle of the upper half of the body in the previous frame is multiplied by the values of pixels in the area above the horizontal line passing through CoG. Let g_{ij} be the image obtained by this operation. Since areas corresponding to the torso and head are emphasized in

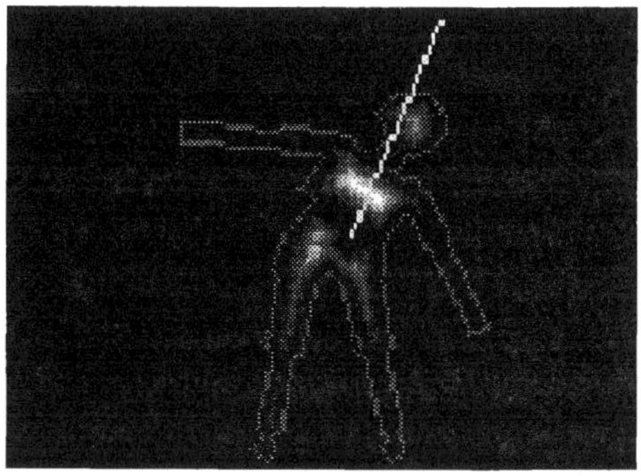

Figure 3.4. g_{ij} image with PAU (the white line)

g_{ij}, while the arm areas are suppressed (Fig. 3.4), the orientation of the upper half of the human body is obtained as the inclination θ of the principal axis of inertia of g_{ij} from the following equation:

$$\tan^2\theta + \frac{\mathrm{M}(2,\,0) - \mathrm{M}(0,\,2)}{\mathrm{M}(1,\,1)}\tan\theta - 1 = 0 \tag{3.4}$$

where

$$\mathrm{M}(p,\,q) = \sum_i \sum_j (i - I_c)^p (j - J_c)^q g_{ij}.$$

In Fig. 3.4, θ is the angle between the principal axis of the upper body (PAU) and the vertical line.

3.2.2.3 Locating Significant Points. After preprocessing is performed, tips of the feet and hands, and the top of the head are located as significant points.

(1) Preprocess

In the silhouette image f_{ij}, the contour of the human silhouette is obtained from a border tracking technique. Significant points, more specifically, the tips of the feet, the tips of the hands, and the top of the head, need to be located from the contour.

As a preprocess, the CoG of the upper half of the body image g_{ij}, UCoG, is obtained by using Eqs. (3.1) and (3.2) for the pixels in the area above the horizontal line passing through CoG. Then, the principal axis of the upper body (PAU) is obtained as the line that passes through UCoG and is parallel to the orientation of the upper body. A temporary location for top of the head is chosen. This point is the contour pixel nearest to PAU and farthest above

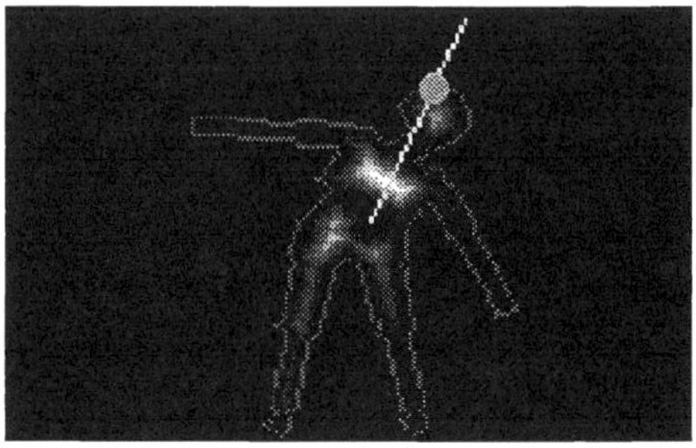

Figure 3.5. Finding the temporary position of the head (the circle in this figure)

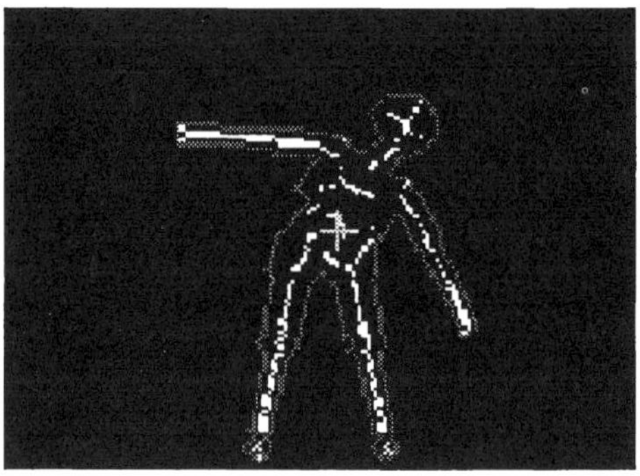

Figure 3.6. Local maxima of a skeleton image (white pixels)

the UCoG. As shown in Fig. 3.5, normally, the point at which PAU and the contour intersect is chosen as the temporary top of the head.

(2) Tips of Feet

A skeleton image (Fig. 3.6) is created by connecting local maxima of distance-transformed image d_{ij}. This skeleton image includes many edge (or end) points, which are candidates for the tips of the feet. As shown in Fig. 3.7, the tips of the feet are chosen from the the foot candidates that satisfy the following conditions: (1) they are located in the lower half of the body (below CoG), and (2) they are farthest from the CoG to the left and right, respectively.

(3) Tips of Hands

As shown in Fig. 3.8, the contour pixels ranging between the temporary location of the top of the head and the tip of the foot is divided into three segments by predetermined pixel number ratio $l_{\mathrm{h}} : m_{\mathrm{h}} : n_{\mathrm{h}}$, which is useful for most humans. The middle segment, corresponding to the ratio m_{h}, is the hand candidate contour segment. In this segment, the hand candidate points **A**, **B** and

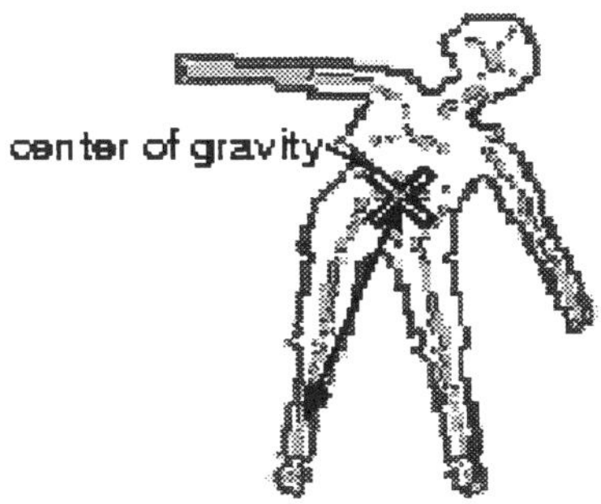

Figure 3.7. Locating tip of foot

C are chosen, where **A** is at the highest position in the vertical direction, **B** is at the lowest, **C** is at the farthest from the CoG. Next, the following conditions are evaluated one after the other to obtain the tip of the hand. If a condition is satisfied, then the candidate satisfying it is chosen, otherwise the next condition is evaluated. Each condition assumes the 2D coordinate system whose origin is the lower-left corner of an image and whose two axes are the horizontal and vertical directions of the image; thereby, upper and right coordinates take large values.

1 If (vertical position of candidate **A**) $>$ (vertical position of the temporary of head top) $- T_1$, then **A**.

2 If (vertical position of candidate **B**) $<$ (vertical position of CoG) $+ T_1$, then **B**.

3 If (horizontal position of candidate **C**) $<$ (horizontal position of CoG) $+ T_2$ (for the right hand; for the left hand, $<$ is replaced by $>$), then **C**.

4 Otherwise, the lower end point of the hand candidate contour segment (i.e., the hand is down, alongside the body).

In the above four conditions, T_1 and T_2 are constant values, which are determined based on the height of the rectangle enclosing the body silhouette region during the initial calibration (Fig. 3.1).

(4) Top of the Head

The contour pixels ranging between the temporary top of the head location and the tip of the hand is divided into three segments by a predetermined ratio $l_{\mathrm{p}} : m_{\mathrm{p}} : n_{\mathrm{p}}$. It can be considered that the middle segments for the left and right hand tips include the left and right neck sides, respectively. Each neck side pixel is chosen as the contour pixel that has the shortest distance to the

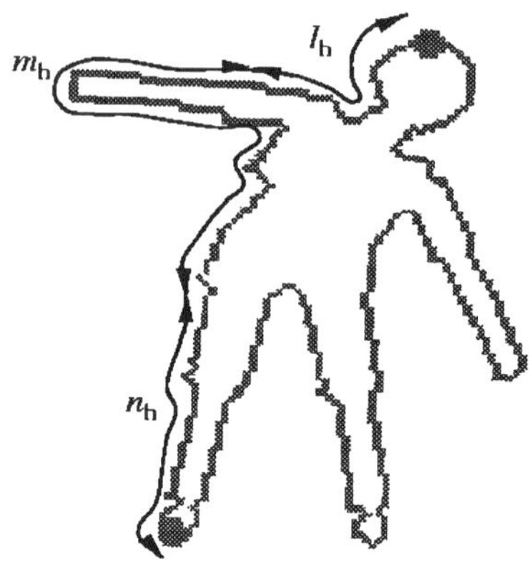

Figure 3.8. Contour segments to locate the tip of the hand

principal axis, PAU. Then, the central (middle) point between both neck side points along the contour is determined as the top of the head.

3.2.3. Estimating Major Joint Positions

To reproduce the entire posture of a person, the information such as the positions of the center of gravity, the head, the hands, or the foot are not enough. We also need the position data for major joints such as elbows and knees. However, these positions do not always have salient features in the contour of the silhouette (e.g., like the posture in Figs. 3.3 to 3.6, where the arms are stretched), thus heuristic methods are not useful.

We estimate the elbow and knee positions from the located positions of the significant points by a learning procedure based on the genetic algorithm (GA) [Goldberg, 1989]

3.2.3.1 A GA Based Estimation Algorithm. The positions of the elbows and knees are represented by linear combinations of the positions of the significant points. As explained in Sections 3.2.3.2 and 3.2.3.3, there are quite many coefficients to be determined in the linear combination equations.

In such a case, finding the values of the coefficients is a combinatorial optimization problem, and GA is appropriate for solving this type of problem. In GA, candidate solutions of a problem are represented as genes of chromosome of each individual in a population. The initial chromosome population is generated at random, and some genetic operations such as crossover and mutation are stochastically applied to each individual so that individuals that fit well to the environment can survive at high probabilities. After a large number of the cycles, the gene data of the individual with the best fitness are considered as solutions.

The coefficients of the linear combinations are assigned to genes of each individual, and the coefficient value combination that minimizes the estimation error is searched for by GA. Training image data for a variety of human postures are collected, and the positions of the major joints in each training image are located manually. In the GA procedure, each training data corresponds to an individual.

Let x_i and $\hat{x}_i$ be the real and estimated values of the horizontal joint positions, respectively, in the ith image of the training data. The fitness (evaluation function) f are defined by the following equation:

$$\frac{1}{f} = \bar{e} + \frac{1}{k}\sum_{i=1}^{k}(x_i - \hat{x}_i - \bar{e})^2 \tag{3.5}$$

where

$$\bar{e} = \frac{1}{k}\sum_{i=1}^{k} x_i - \hat{x}_i$$

In Eq.(3.5), k denotes the number of major joints.

3.2.3.2 Elbow Joint Position. The following equations (Eqs.(3.6) and (3.7)) show how to estimate the position of the elbow using the positions of the center of gravity of the body $(x_{\mathrm{g}}, y_{\mathrm{g}})$, the top of the head $(x_{\mathrm{p}}, y_{\mathrm{p}})$, the tip of the hand $(x_{\mathrm{h}}, y_{\mathrm{h}})$ and the tip of the foot $(x_{\mathrm{f}}, y_{\mathrm{f}})$. Here, coordinate values are with respect to CoG, like $\tilde{x} = x - x_{\mathrm{g}}$.

$$\tilde{x}_{\mathrm{e}} = C_1\,(x_{\mathrm{h}} - x_{\mathrm{p}}) + C_2\,(y_{\mathrm{h}} - y_{\mathrm{p}}) + C_3\,\tilde{x}_{\mathrm{h}} + C_4\,\tilde{y}_{\mathrm{h}} + C_5 \tag{3.6}$$
$$\tilde{y}_{\mathrm{e}} = C_6\,(x_{\mathrm{h}} - x_{\mathrm{p}}) + C_7\,(y_{\mathrm{h}} - y_{\mathrm{p}}) + C_8\,\tilde{x}_{\mathrm{h}} + C_9\,\tilde{y}_{\mathrm{h}} + C_{10} \tag{3.7}$$

The coefficients C_i of Eqs. (3.6) and (3.7) are to be estimated by the GA procedure. In Eqs. (3.6) and (3.7), when the coordinates of the left elbow are calculated, the coordinates of the tip of the left hand and the tip of the left foot are used. Similarly, the coordinates of the right elbow are calculated.

3.2.3.3 Knee Joint Position. Before estimating the knee position, we search for the contour point $(x_{\mathrm{l}}, y_{\mathrm{l}})$, whose vertical position bisects CoG and the tip of foot. The knee position $(x_{\mathrm{k}}, y_{\mathrm{k}})$ is computed as follows:

$$\tilde{x}_{\mathrm{k}} = W_1\,\tilde{x}_{\mathrm{p}} + W_2\,\tilde{y}_{\mathrm{p}} + W_3\,\tilde{x}_{\mathrm{f}} + W_4\,\tilde{y}_{\mathrm{f}} + W_5\,\tilde{x}_{\mathrm{l}} + W_6\,\tilde{y}_{\mathrm{l}} + W_7 \tag{3.8}$$

$$\tilde{y}_{\mathrm{k}} = W_8\,\tilde{x}_{\mathrm{p}} + W_9\,\tilde{y}_{\mathrm{p}} + W_{10}\,\tilde{x}_{\mathrm{f}} + W_{11}\,\tilde{y}_{\mathrm{f}} + W_{12}\,\tilde{x}_{\mathrm{l}} + W_{13}\,\tilde{y}_{\mathrm{l}} + W_{14} \tag{3.9}$$

Similarly, the coefficients W_i in Eqs.(3.8) and (3.9) are estimated by the GA procedure.

3.2.4. Experimental Results and Discussions

3.2.4.1 Experimental System. The proposed method is implemented on a workstation (SGI Indy R4400/100MHz). Thermal images are acquired from an infrared CCD camera (Nikon Thermal Vision LAIRD3). This infrared camera with 27 mm focal length lens has the ability to observe thermal range from -20 to 50 ℃, and its measurement error caused by thermal noise is smaller than 0.15 ℃ at 27 ℃ black body radiation. The thermal images are captured and digitized at 160 by 120 pixel resolution and 8 bit temperature depth.

3.2.4.2 Significant Point Location Results. Before using actual thermal images acquired by the infrared camera, the method was tested on a simple simulation, which generates target images from a 3-D human body model consisting of 200 wire-frame vertices. An orthographic frontal view of the model was used for the computer generated images.

The test results on significant points, shown in Fig. 3.9, show that the proposed method can permit more than 75 degree of PAU angle. This makes it possible to estimate various kinds of postures, because the estimation of PAU directly influences the location of the temporary head top, where wrong location of the temporary head top causes location failure in the hand tips and the real head top. The proposed method can also estimate the posture when the foot is held up high as shown in Fig. 3.9.

The algorithm was tested for real thermal images also. Fig. 3.10 shows some example of the results. In each row of Fig. 3.10, the left and middle columns indicate the original images and the located positions of the significant points, respectively. In the middle column of Fig. 3.10, the small squares indicate the located positions. It turns out that the locations are very accurate.

3.2.4.3 Joint Position Estimation. In order to test our estimation method on elbows and knee joint, the following steps are performed.

Thermal image sequences of postures which involve various motions and angles of elbow and knee joints are shot. These postures include bending an elbow, raising the hands, bending and then extending an elbow, stepping to the side, and raising a foot. The real elbow/knee joint positions are manually acquired. Next, the coefficients, C_i and W_i, are obtained by using GA on

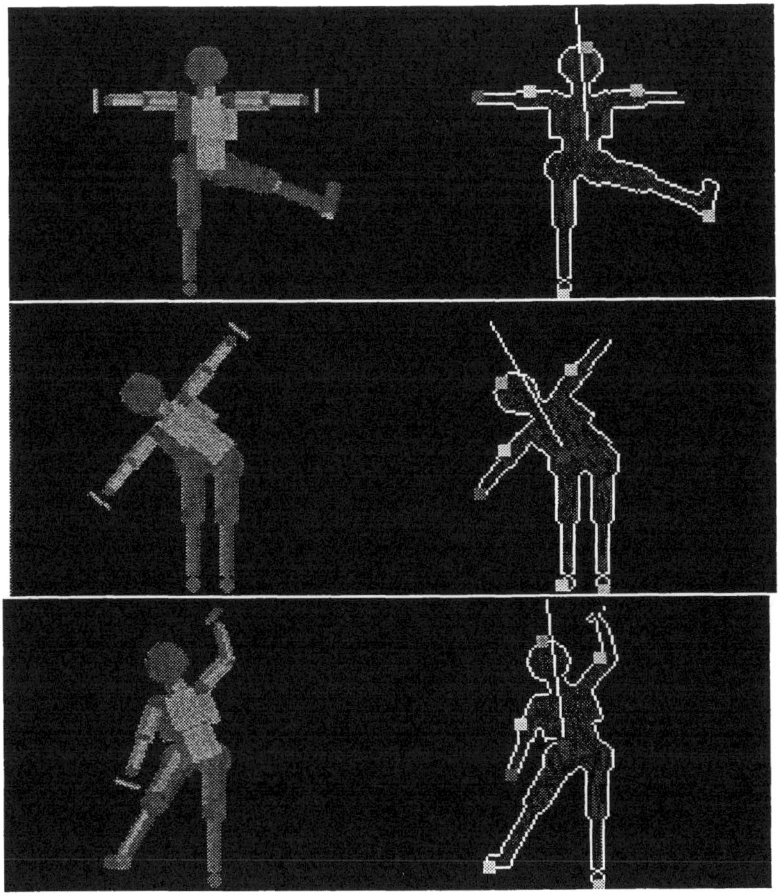

Figure 3.9. Located significant points (target images are generated by using the 3-D human body model)

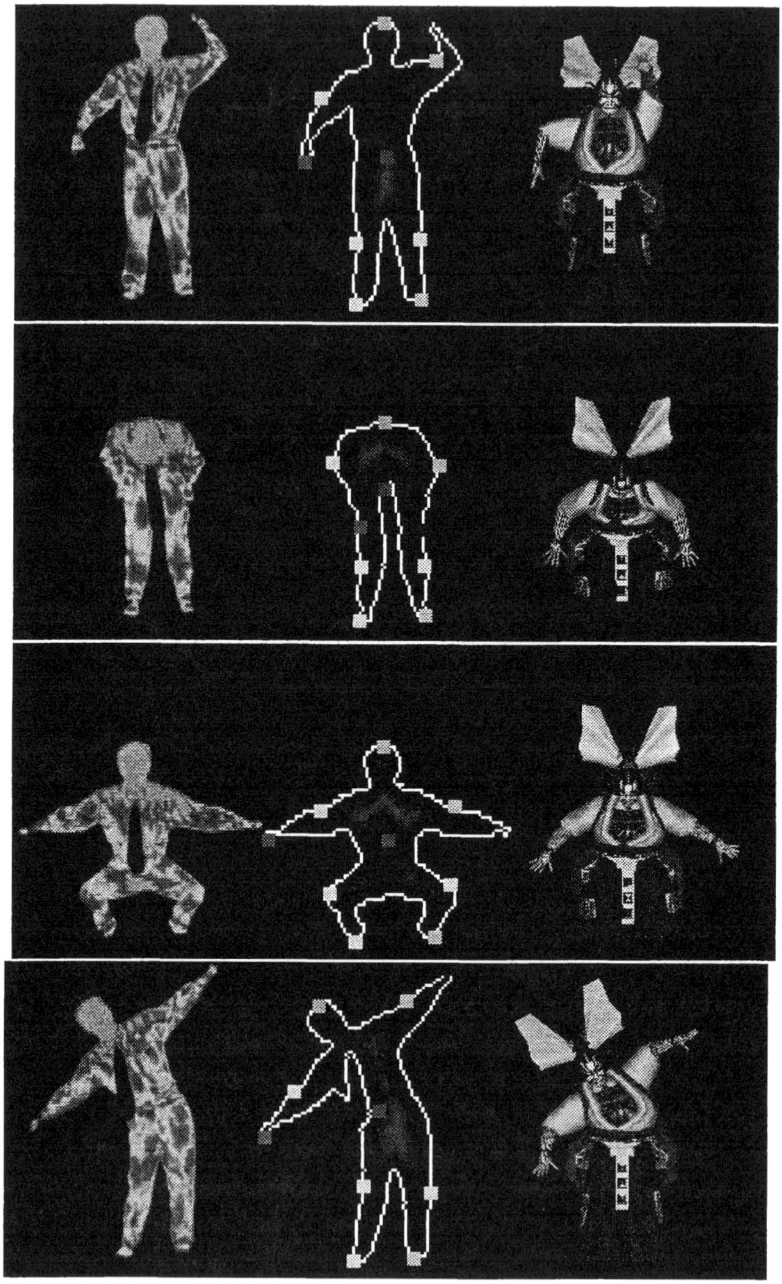

Figure 3.10. Experimental results and reproduced Kabuki characters (left column: original thermal image; middle column: located significant points; right column: reproduction in a Kabuki avatar

Eqs.(3.6) through (3.9) with real positions, respectively. The following GA parameters are applied:

- number of individual: 2000
- number of generation: 3000
- crossover rate: 0.02
- mutation rate: 0.003

We estimate the joint positions using the Eqs. (3.6) through (3.9), whose coefficients have been determined by the GA based procedure, and compare the estimation results with the real positions. In Figs. 3.11 and 3.12, the solid line represents real positions; the dotted line represents estimated positions. The results show that the average estimation error is limited to between one pixel and two pixels, and the estimated positions are good approximation of the real one. As examples of the experimental results for the real images shown in Fig. 3.10, the estimations work very well.

3.2.4.4 Real-time Demonstration. As an evaluation and application of this method, an interactive system [Ohya et al., 1996] was built. In this system, the computer graphics generated 3-D character in which the estimated motions (posture sequences) of the person are reproduced is rendered in real-time. A couple of hundred participants tried to play a character, a Japanese Kabuki actor in this system. Although the background was complicated and the lighting condition were very dark and varied everywhere, the posture estimation was quite stable in real-time. For participants wearing a skirt, it occasionally became unstable due to the low thermal conductivity of clothes.

Some estimation results and the reproduced Kabuki character with corresponding postures are shown in Fig. 3.10. The bowing posture, which is potentially ambiguous in 2D, is correctly reproduced due to some constraints applied to the results. The main constraint for this case is that the human body does not move back and forth along the depth direction. So, if the vertical distance from the CoG to the top of the head is shorter than the calibrated one, it is assumed that the upper body is leaning forward.

The overall processing rate is about 20 frames a second so that quite quick response for visual communications and virtual reality applications is achieved. This system is detailed in Section 3.5.2.

3.2.5. Summary

Section 3.2 presents a method of real-time posture estimation of a human body from a monocular thermal image. In this method, the upper body orientation estimation and heuristic contour analysis are performed on the sil-

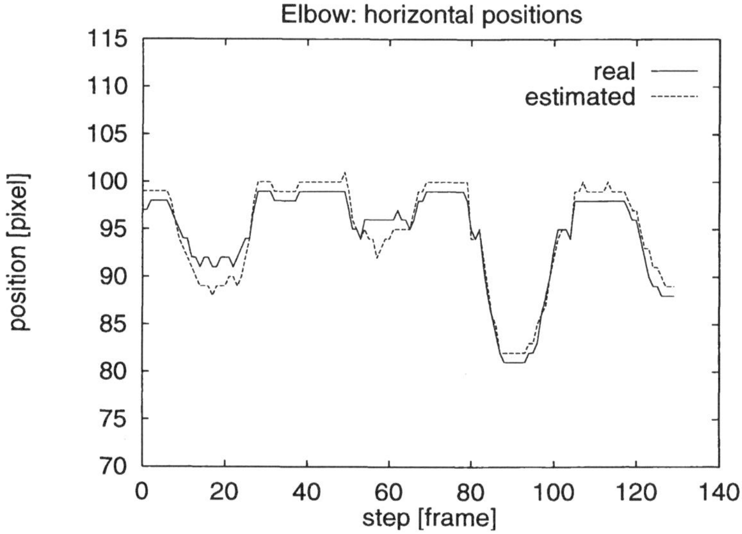

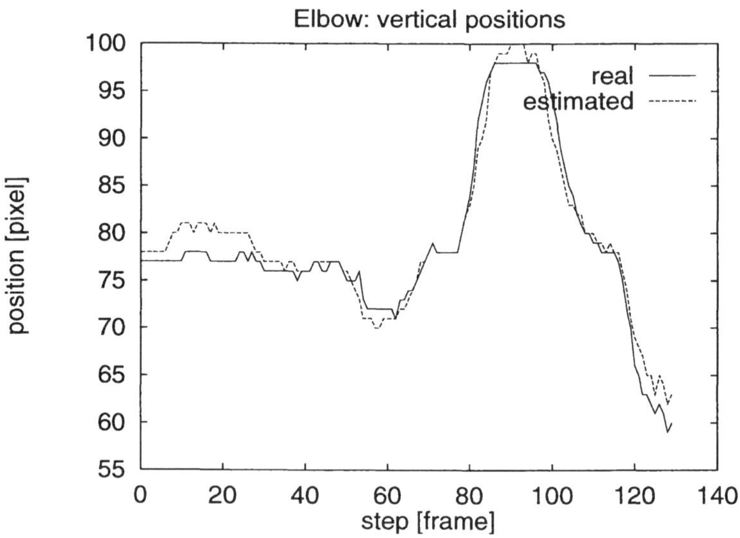

Figure 3.11. Estimation results of an elbow joint position

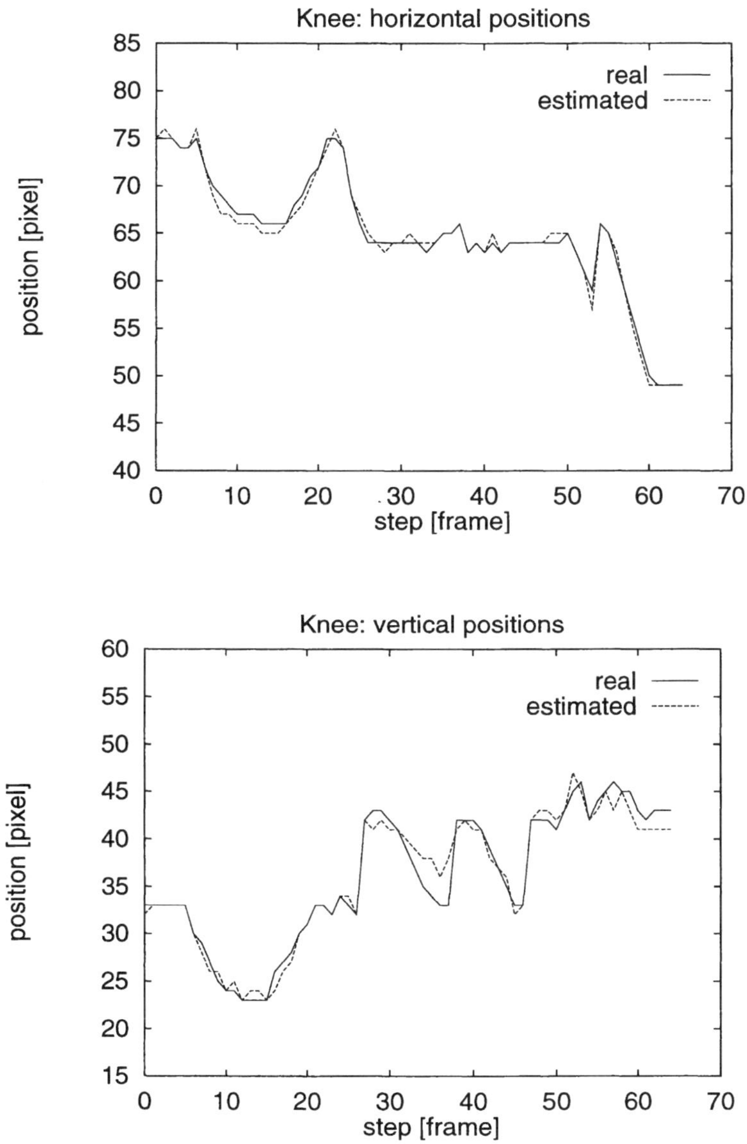

Figure 3.12. Estimation results of a knee joint position

houette obtained from the thermal image. The major joint position estimation technique based on the GA learning procedure has also been developed.

The experimental results show the proposed method works in a robust and stable manner in real-time in spite of difficult lighting and background conditions. The calibration procedure is able to adapt all sorts of physiques. In addition, the GA based major joint position estimation can locate the point where the silhouette contour does not have a salient image feature.

Adaptating to more varied types of clothing is a remaining issue. Another issue includes the extension from 2D posture estimation to 3D posture estimation. These issues could be solved by using multiple color CCD cameras. The following sections describe two approaches.

3.3. A Heuristic Method for Estimating Postures in 3D

3.3.1. Outline

To estimate a person's posture in 3D, multiple cameras should be used to observe the person, as opposed to the 2D posture estimation method described in Section 3.2. Reconstruction from a multiple camera system, however, requires substantial computational cost. Here, for a trade-off between computational cost and estimation accuracy, we use three color CCD cameras that observe the person from the top, front and side. We use the top view to easily estimate the rotation angle of a human body. At given time, the person's posture is estimated in 3D by obtaining the 3D coordinates of significant points such as the top of the head and the elbows from the evaluated 2D coordinates of corresponding points on images acquired by the three cameras.

Our approach is based on the analysis of silhouettes, which correspond to areas occupied by the body in the three images. Silhouettes are typically extracted by calculating the difference at each pixel between the background image and the input image, and thresholding the difference at that pixel. The thresholded image, in which each pixel has a value indicating that the pixel belongs to either the foreground or the background, is called a "silhouette image". Silhouette images can easily be obtained using a background with a uniform color. Recently, quite many promising silhouette extraction methods that can be applied to backgrounds with complex textures have been developed (e.g. [Haritaoglu et al., 1998]). If an infrared camera is used instead of a CCD camera (as in our method described in Section 3.2), the silhouette is extracted by a simple thresholding of the thermal image thus acquired. This section focuses on the processes needed to estimate human postures in 3D from the silhouette images acquired by the three cameras.

The method proposed in this section is outlined in Fig. 3.13. The orientation of the upper half of the body (above the waist) is obtained in each silhouette image after the centroid of the human silhouette is calculated. Then, a heuristic

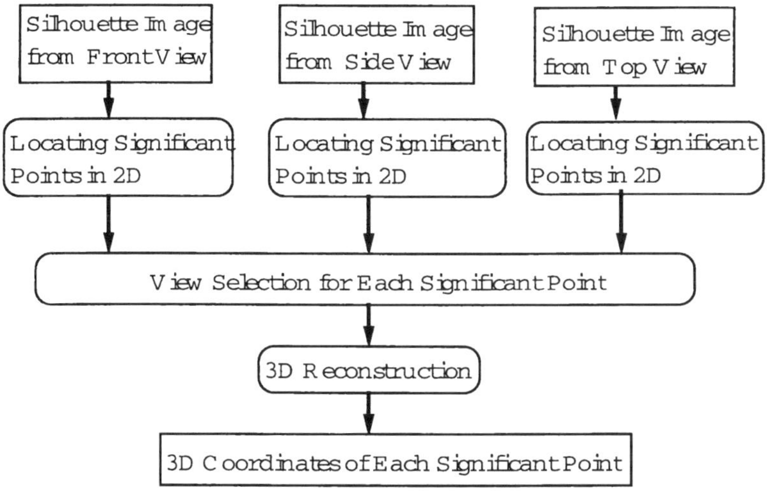

Figure 3.13. Outline of the heuristic method for 3D posture estimation

contour analysis of the silhouette is used to detect the significant points. Based on the detected locations of the significant points, we estimate the positions of the major joints by a learning based procedure. To reconstruct 3D coordinates of the significant points, we select two views by evaluating the appropriateness of each located significant point in the three views. We use the two views to calculate the 3D coordinates of each significant point by triangulation.

In fact, the process described in Section 3.2 is used to locate significant points in the front and side images. Therefore, only the process applied to the top view image is described in the following section.

3.3.2. Image Processing for Top Camera

3.3.2.1 Rotation Angle of the Body. In the image acquired by the top camera, the rotation angle ϕ of the body is estimated, where ϕ indicates the direction the torso is facing. The principal axis (PA) is used to estimate the rotation angle ϕ, where the PA in the top image is obtained by the same process used to obtain PAU's in the front and side images (Section 3.2.2.2). As show in Fig. 3.14, the rotation angle ϕ is defined as the angle between PA and the horizontal direction, and is measured counterclockwise from the horizontal direction. By using Eq. (3.4) for the top image, we obtain four temporary PA's. These temporary PA's are four vectors whose origin is the CoG, and each PA is oriented in one of the four different directions along two orthogonal lines passing through the CoG. The temporary PA whose orientation is closest to that of the PA in the previous frame is chosen as the PA in the current frame, where the initial PA is determined as the orientation of the left arm orientation in the initial calibration pose (Fig. 3.15).

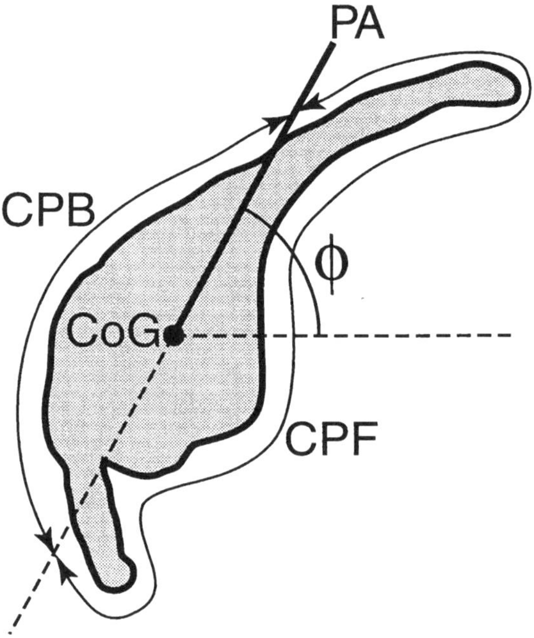

Figure 3.14. Principal Axis (PA) and Contour in the Top View

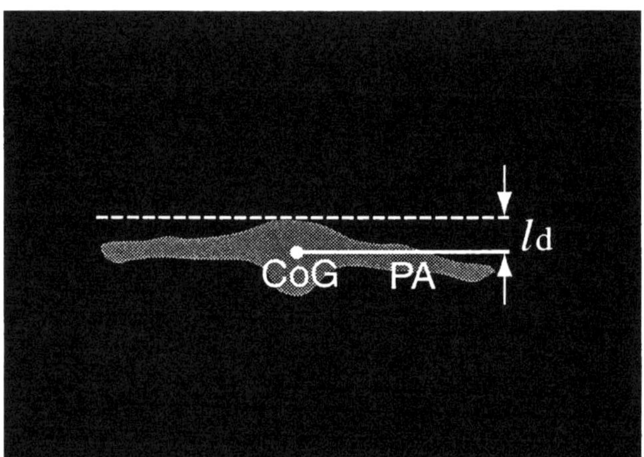

Figure 3.15. Posture for Initial Calibration in the Top View

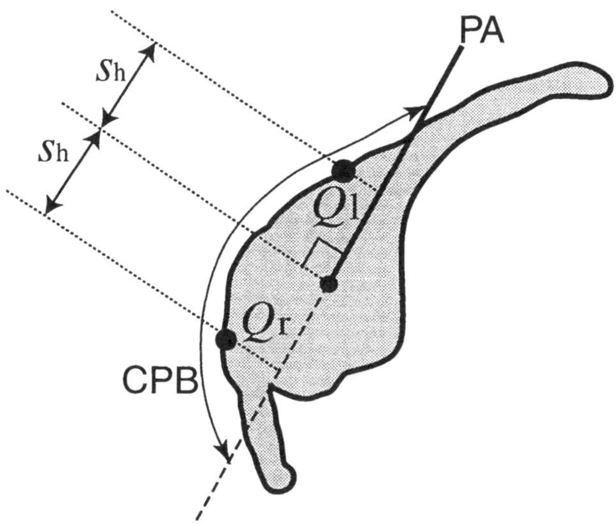

Figure 3.16. Candidate for the Top of the Head in the Top View

The contour of the silhouette in the top view image is obtained by a border tracking algorithm. As shown in Fig. 3.14, the segment of contour pixels in the region of $[\phi, \pi + \phi]$ is called CPB (contour pixels of the back of the body), and that in the region of $[\pi + \phi, 2\pi + \phi]$ are called CPF (contour pixels of the front of the body).

3.3.2.2 Significant Points. In the top image, each significant point is located as follows.

(1) The Top of the Head:

The candidate contour segment that inlcudes the top of the head is assumed to be the region between two points, $\boldsymbol{Q}_\mathrm{r}$ and $\boldsymbol{Q}_\mathrm{l}$ in the CPB, as shown in Fig. 3.16. In Fig. 3.16, $\boldsymbol{Q}_\mathrm{r}(\boldsymbol{Q}_\mathrm{l})$ are the intersections of the CPB and the lines perpendicular to the PA that are at a distance s_h to the right or left of the CoG, respectively. In the candidate contour segment, the farthest position from the PA is chosen as the top of the head.

(2) The Tips of Feet:

The candidate contour segment for the tip of the right or left foot is assumed to be the region between two points, $\boldsymbol{U}$ and $\boldsymbol{V}$, in the CPF, as shown in Fig. 3.17. $\boldsymbol{U}$ is at the nearest position from the CoG in the CPF. $\boldsymbol{V}$ is the intersection of the CPF and the line perpendicular to the PA at a distance s_f from the CoG on the same side as the foot. For each candidate contour segment, the farthest position from the PAU is chosen as the tip of the foot.

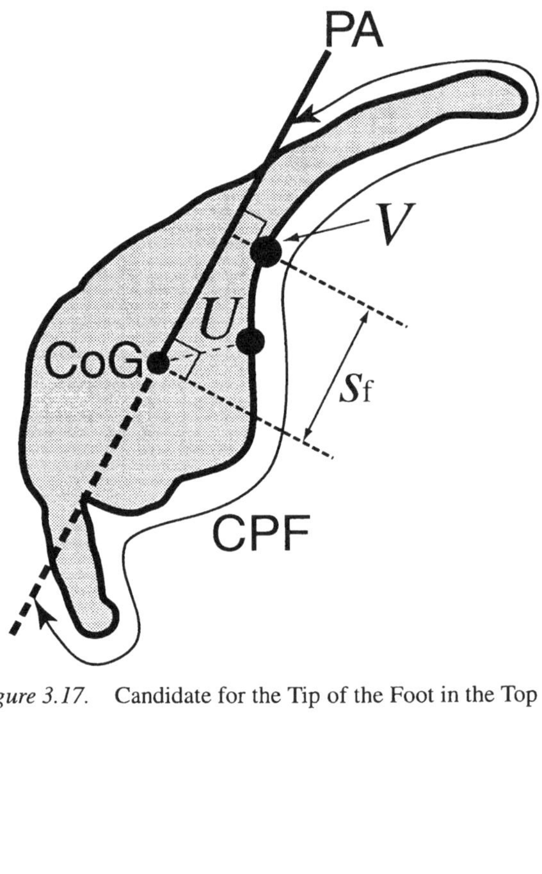

Figure 3.17. Candidate for the Tip of the Foot in the Top View

(3) The Tips of Hands:

As shown in Fig. 3.18, the contours between the top of the head and the tips of the feet are divided into two segments by a predetermined pixel number ratio $l_{\mathrm{q}} : m_{\mathrm{q}}$ (in our current implementation, $l_{\mathrm{q}} : m_{\mathrm{q}} = 1 : 4$). The segment, corresponding to the ratio m_{q}, is assumed to be the hand candidate contour segment. In the hand candidate contour segment, three hand candidate points $\boldsymbol{P}_{\mathrm{A}}$, $\boldsymbol{P}_{\mathrm{B}}$, and $\boldsymbol{P}_{\mathrm{C}}$ are chosen, where $\boldsymbol{P}_{\mathrm{A}}$ is the point whose distance from PA, l_{PA}, is the largest in the hand candidate contour segment in CPF. $\boldsymbol{P}_{\mathrm{B}}$ is the end point of the hand candidate contour segment which starts at the top of the head in the CPF; $\boldsymbol{P}_{\mathrm{C}}$ is the point whose distance, l_{PC}, from the line that is perpendicular to the PA and passes through the CoG is the largest in the hand tip contour segment. Similarly, the three candidate points for the other hand are obtained.

The following conditions are evaluated one after the other to locate the tip of the hand. If a condition is satisfied, then the candidate satisfying the condition is chosen, otherwise the next condition is evaluated.

1 If $l_{PC} > T_3$, then P_C.

2 If $l_{PA} > T_4$, then P_A.

3 Otherwise, P_B.

Here T_3 and T_4 are constant values that are determined from the maximal distance, l_d, between PA and CPB in the initial calibration (Fig. 3.15). Our implementation uses $T_3 = T_4 = 2.0 l_d$.

3.3.3. Estimating Major Joint Positions

As described in Section 3.2.3, to reproduce the entire posture of an individual, we need not only the positions of the centroid, the head, the hands, and the feet, but also the positions of major joints such as the elbows and knees. However, these positions do not always have salient image features in the contour of their silhouettes (e.g. in the case of the stretched arm). Therefore, similar to the method described in Section 3.2.3, we estimate the elbow and knee positions from the located positions of the significant points using a learning procedure based on a genetic algorithm (GA) [Goldberg, 1989]. That is, in each of the three images, the positions of the elbows and knees are represented by linear combinations of the positions of the significant points, and then the coefficients of the linear combinations are determined by the GA based learning procedure (Eqs. (3.6) through (3.9)). To estimate the position of the elbows and knees, the positions of the significant points are substituted into the linear combinations, whose coefficients have been determined.

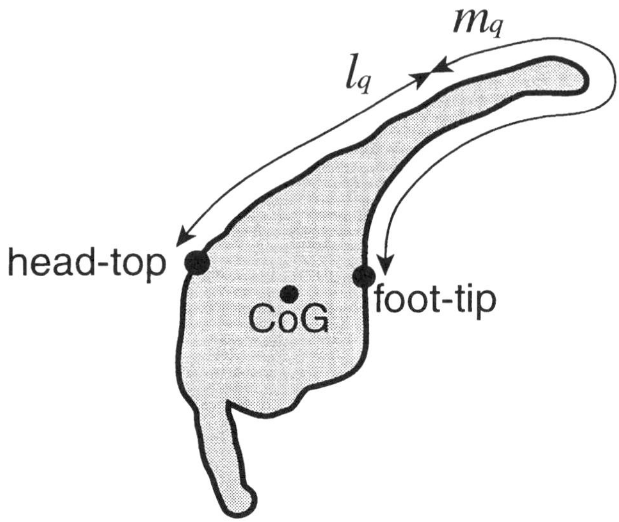

Figure 3.18. Candidate for Hand Tip in the Top View

3.3.4. 3D Reconstruction of the Significant Points

To reconstruct the 3D coordinates of each significant point, two views are sufficient if the points can be located in both views. In our method, however, we use three cameras from different directions to reduce the probability of occlusion. Even if occlusion occurs in one of the three images, 3D reconstruction can be achieved from the other two. Therefore, our basic strategy is to obtain the 3D coordinates of each significant point by selecting two appropriate views that avoid occlusion.

The appropriateness of views is evaluated for each significant point based on the algorithms for locating them. For example, in the algorithm for locating the tips of the hands (Sections 3.2.2.3 and 3.3.2.2), the conditions 1. to 4. (1. to 3. in the top view) are evaluated in order. When one of the conditions is satisfied, the location process is finished. Conditions 1. and 4. (1. and 3. in the top view) have the highest and lowest priorities, respectively. This priority is checked for the three views, and the two views with the highest and second highest priorities are selected. Similar rules are applied to the other significant points. As a result, two appropriate views are different for the significant points. In Section 3.3.5.2, we will explain which views are selected to locate significant points in details. Note that the front and side views are always used to locate the CoG and the top of the head. The rotation angle of the human body is detected from the top view.

The 3D coordinates of each significant point are calculated with the 2D coordinates of the located significant point in the two selected views, with the triangulation principle based on the camera parameters of the three cameras and the geometrical relationships between the three cameras.

3.3.5. Experimental Results and Discussions

3.3.5.1 Experimental System. The proposed method was coded in the C++ language and implemented on a personal computer (dual Pentium II 400MHz running Windows NT 4.0). Three cameras observe the person from the front, side and top. we used green colored background, which allows a fast and accurate extraction of the silhouette images. The silhouette is extracted from the background using chroma keyers. The silhouette images from the three CCD cameras are synchronously input into the computer and are digitized at the 160 by 120 pixel resolution. The entire process of estimating human postures in 3D runs at a speed of 30 Hz, which is the same as a video rate.

3.3.5.2 Significant Point Detection Results. Figures 3.19, 3.20 and 3.21 show examples of the original images from the three directions, the silhouettes of the original trinocular images and the locations of the significant points in each image, respectively. In Fig. 3.21, the small squares indicate the located position of each significant point. As described in Section 3.3.4, two appropriate views are selected for each significant point before the 3D coordinates of the significant points are calculated. In Fig. 3.21, the tip of the right hand is located using the side and top images while the tip of the left hand is located using the front and top images.

To confirm the effectiveness of the proposed method, we conducted the following experiment. A person was requested to assume a sequence of different postures, which were recorded by the three cameras. We applied our method to each frame of the recorded sequences, and the 2D coordinates of the significant points were estimated. The real locations of the significant points in the three views at each frame were also obtained manually and stored.

We compared the results obtained by selecting the two appropriate views and simply using the three views. In the former (the proposed method), we averaged the distance between the real and estimated locations of each significant point in the two selected views; in the latter (non-selection method), we averaged the distance between the real and estimated locations over the three views. The average errors using the proposed method are: 5.0 pixels in the top of the head, 5.8 pixels in the tip of the right hand, and 4.9 pixels in the tip of the right foot. On the other hand, the errors using three views are: 9.5 pixels, 13.7 pixels and 9.3 pixels, respectively. This result shows that the selection

Figure 3.19. Original Trinocular Images (upper-left: front view, upper-right: side view, lower-left: top view, lower-right: no image)

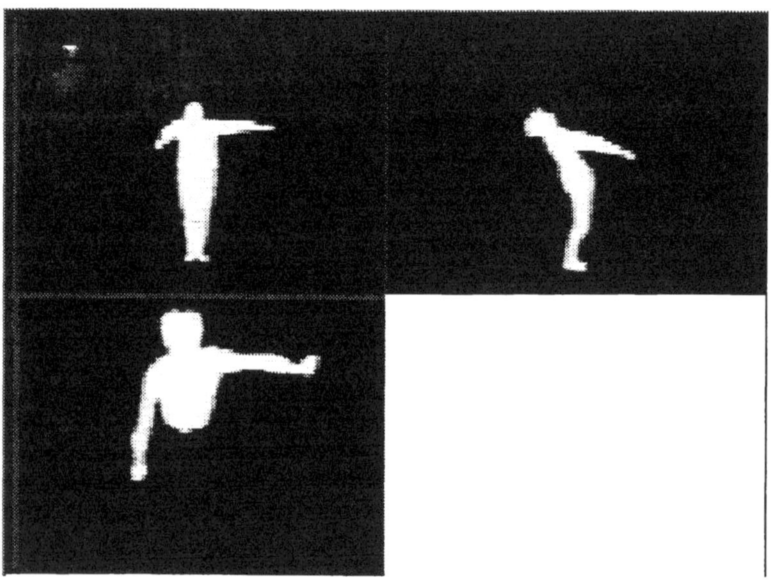

Figure 3.20. Silhouettes of the Original Trinocular Images

Figure 3.21. Results of Locating Significant Points in the Trinocular Images

method gives better results. Overall, similar results were obtained for the other significant points.

3.3.6. Summary

Section 3.3 presents a real-time heuristic method for estimating human postures in 3D from trinocular images. In this method, the upper body orientation detection and a heuristic contour analysis are performed on the human silhouettes in the trinocular images. The major joint positions are estimated by a genetic algorithm based learning procedure. Then, the 3D coordinates of significant points that represent human postures are obtained from the two selected views.

The method in this section is implemented on a personal computer, and the process runs in real-time (30 frames per second). Experimental results show that the estimation accuracy of this approach is quite high. It turns out that the view selection method gives more accurate results than the non-view-selection method.

The proposed method utilizes silhouettes. Therefore, it is difficult to deal with postures that cause self-occlusions in all three images. Useful image features other than human silhouettes should also be studied so that arbitrary postures can be accurately estimated. In addition, one of the most serious problems of this method is lack of its generality: i.e. there are many postures that cannot be dealt with by this heuristic approach. The next section describes a method that can overcome some of these limitations.

3.4. A Non-heuristic Method for Estimating Postures in 3D

3.4.1. Outline

The method for 3D posture estimation in Section 3.3 runs in real-time. However, postures that can be estimated by this method are limited, because the approach utilizes heuristic rules and empirical knowledge about the dimensions and proportions of the body. For example, it is assumed that the tip of the right foot is always on the right side of the body below the horizontal midline, likewise the left hand is always on the upper left side. Examples of postures this method cannot estimate include the right hand moved to the left side of the body, or an arm and leg crossing each other. This section describes a method that can estimate such postures without using the above-mentioned heuristic rules or empirical knowledge.

Similar to the method in Section 3.3, we use three color CCD cameras, which observe a person from the top, front and side. Figure 3.22 shows the world coordinate system, $X - Y - Z$. The 2D coordinate system $x - y$ for each image is defined such that the origin of $x - y$ is at the lower-left corner of the image, and the x and y axes are the horizontal and vertical directions, respectively. By using the top view, the rotation angle of the human body can be detected. At a given point in time, posture is estimated in 3D by obtaining the 3D coordinates of significant points (i.e., the op of the head, and the tips of the hands and feet) taken from the estimated 2D coordinates of the corresponding points in the images captured by the three cameras.

In each image, significant points are located using a function analysis on contours of human silhouettes. In this case, we assume that self-occlusions do not occur in the human silhouettes. When self-occlusions do occur, on the other hand, difference images between the present and previous frame images are used to locate the significant points. The time series for each significant point is approximated with an autoregressive model (AR model) to track the position of the significant point and to predict its position N steps ahead of the current image. The predicted position is used as the center of the search area in which difference image is calculated. Here, the parameters of the AR model are estimated by using the Kalman filter, whose input is the located significant points in the present frame.

3.4.2. Locating Significant Points for Each Image

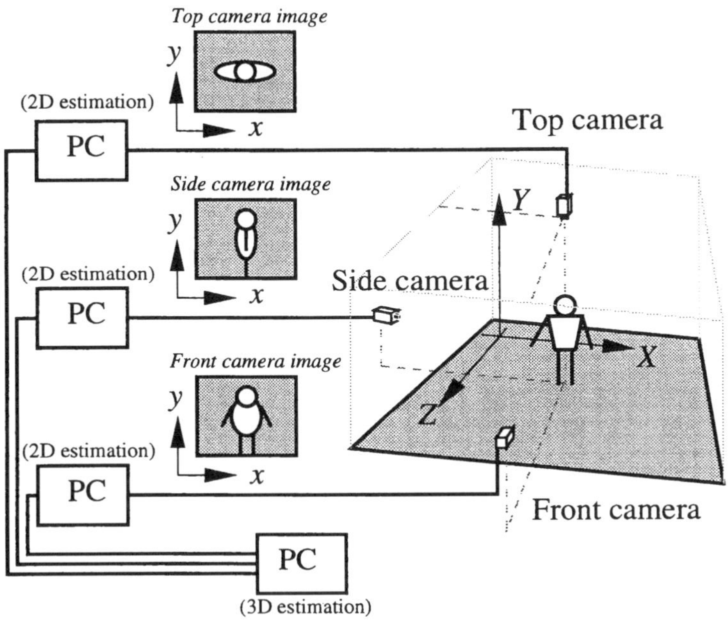

Figure 3.22. Trinocular camera system

3.4.2.1 Contour analysis. First, the needed preprocessing for the function analysis of silhouette contours is performed. Using Eqs. (3.1) through (3.4), the centroid of the silhouette, $[x^g{}_t, y^g{}_t]$ (where t denotes the frame number) is calculated, and the principal axis of the upper half of the body (PAU) is obtained as the inclination θ_t of the silhouette's principal axis of inertia. The contour of the silhouette is then obtained by a border tracking technique.

This contour is analyzed using the function described below to automatically locate significant points (that is, without using the heuristic rules or empirical knowledge described in Section 3.4.1). As shown in Fig. 3.23, we obtain the point P, the intersection of the PAU and the contour. The point series s is defined as the sequence of contour pixels counted from P in the counter-clockwise direction. Let A $[x_t(s), y_t(s)]$ be a point on the contour and and G be the centroid of the human silhouette. Two vectors $\boldsymbol{p}_t(s) = \overrightarrow{AP}$ and $\boldsymbol{g}_t(s) = \overrightarrow{AG}$ are defined. Then, we can define a one-to-one mapping between the geometrical information of the contour image and the point series s by using the following function.

$$L_t(s) = \sqrt{\boldsymbol{p}_t^2(s) + \boldsymbol{g}_t^2(s)} \tag{3.10}$$

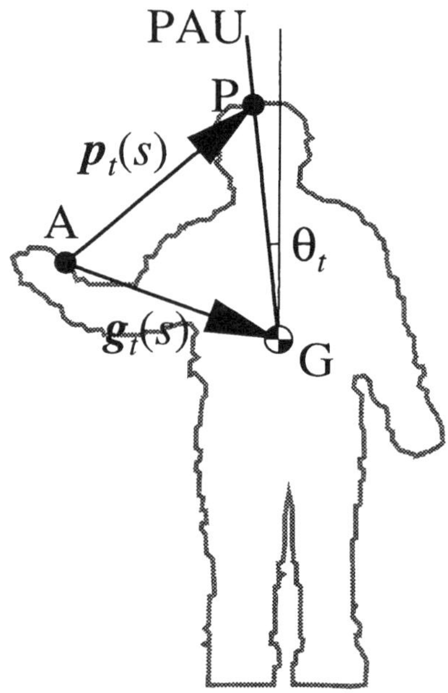

Figure 3.23. Definition of $L_t - s$ curve

Figure 3.24 shows examples of the relationship between the series s and the function output (hereafter called an $L_t - s$ curve) for several postures. By applying an $L_t - s$ curve analysis to various human body postures, we can confirm that the local maximum points of the $L_t - s$ curve correspond to significant points of the human body (white squares in Fig. 3.24 indicate significant points). Accordingly, the locations of the significant points can be obtained by the $L_t - s$ curve analysis. Figure 3.25 compares the $L_t - s$ curve with $k-$curvature and $\Phi - S$ curve. Point A's $k-$curvature is defined as the angle between the line passing through A ($[x_t(s), y_t(s)]$) and point A_{+k} ($[x_t(s+k), y_t(s+k)]$) and the line passing through A and point A_{-k} ($[x_t(s-k), y_t(s-k)]$), where $k = 20$ in Fig. 3.25. In $\Phi - S$ curve, Φ is defined using Fig. 3.23 as the angle between the tangent at point P and the tangent at point A, and S is the distance between point P and point A. As can be seen in Fig. 3.25 (d) and (e), points in which $k-$curvature or Φ changes are supposed to correspond to significant points, but it is difficult to locate the significant points in the curves for $k-$curvature and for $\Phi - S$. On the other hand, the $L_t - s$ curve looks reasonably smooth, and it can be said that robust and easy location of significant points is expected.

The $L_t - s$ curve analysis does not always give information on which local maximum point corresponds to which significant point. For instance, a local maximum in the $L_t - s$ curve might be assigned to significant points in the order of the series s, but postures like those in Fig. 3.24(c), (d), (e) and (h) cannot achieve correct assignments. Therefore, by using the initial calibration posture (Fig. 3.24(a)) before starting the location procedure, we assign the local maximum points to significant points of the human body. In the subsequent frames, significant points are tracked;therefore, the method in this section does not require empirical knowledge about the human body and heuristic rules to locate the significant points.

3.4.2.2 The tracking process using Kalman filter and subtraction image processing. The order of local maxima (significant points) in the $L_t - s$ curve could change according to different postures. For example, in the case of the postures in Fig. 3.24 (a) and (c), the order of significant points in (a) is the right hand, the right foot, the left foot, the left hand and the top of the head. While in (c) it is the top of the head, the right foot, the left foot, the right hand, and the left hand. During a transition from (a) to (c), self-occlusion could occur (where a significant point disappears from the silhouette for a period of time), because the right hand crosses the torso. Since only the contours of the silhoutte images are utilized in $L_t - s$ curve analysis, such analysis cannot deal with self-occlusions. In case of self-occlusions, our method exploits image difference, in which two successive frames (images) are subtracted and thresholded so that a region having large color (brightness) difference between the two images is extracted. To keep tracking a significant point regardless of changes in the order of significant points and self-occlusions, our method applies a Kalman filter to $L_t - s$ curve analysis and image difference.

To optimize and track the positions of the significant points, we assume the AR model for every such point as follows.

$$\boldsymbol{\Psi}_t = \boldsymbol{\Gamma}_t \boldsymbol{\Xi}_t + \boldsymbol{d}\boldsymbol{\epsilon}_t \qquad (3.11)$$

where

$$\begin{aligned}
\boldsymbol{\Psi}_t &= [\Psi_t^{pT} \Psi_t^{hrT} \Psi_t^{hlT} \Psi_t^{frT} \Psi_t^{flT}]^T, \\
\boldsymbol{\Xi}_t &= [\xi_t^{pT} \xi_t^{hrT} \xi_t^{hlT} \xi_t^{frT} \xi_t^{flT}]^T, \\
\boldsymbol{\Gamma}_t &= diag[\boldsymbol{C}_t^p \boldsymbol{C}_t^{hr} \boldsymbol{C}_t^{hl} \boldsymbol{C}_t^{fr} \boldsymbol{C}_t^{fl}], \\
\boldsymbol{C}_t{}^j &= \begin{bmatrix} -x_{t-1}^j & -x_{t-2}^j & \cdots & -x_{t-\rho}^j & 0 & 0 & \cdots & 0 \\ 0 & 0 & \cdots & 0 & -y_{t-1}^j & -y_{t-2}^j & \cdots & -y_{t-\rho}^j \end{bmatrix} \\
\boldsymbol{\Xi}_t^{jT} &= [\ a_1^j \ \ a_2^j \ \ \ldots \ \ a_\rho^j \ \ b_1^j \ \ b_2^j \ \ \ldots \ \ b_\rho^j \ ]
\end{aligned}$$

$\Psi_t^{jT} = [x_t^j y_t^j]$, $j = p$ (top of the head), hl (tip of the left hand), hr (tip of the right hand), fl (tip of the left foot), and fr (tip of the right foot); ρ is the order of the AR model, a_i^j and b_i^j are the unknown parameters, and ϵ_t is the

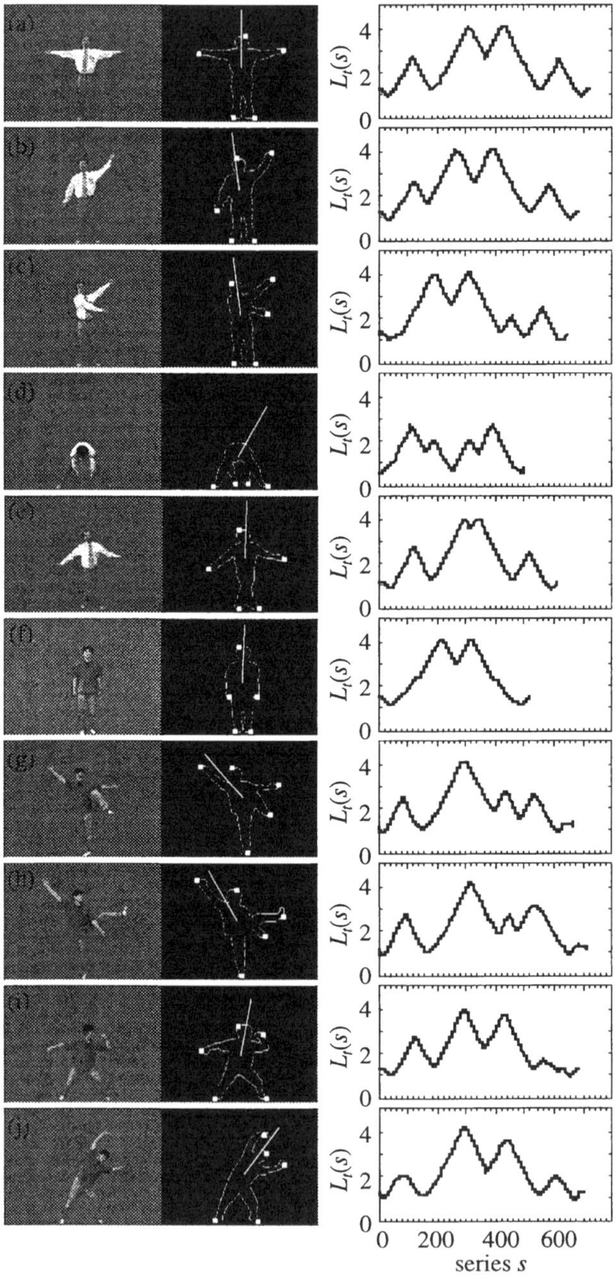

Figure 3.24. Examples of $L_t - s$ curve analysis

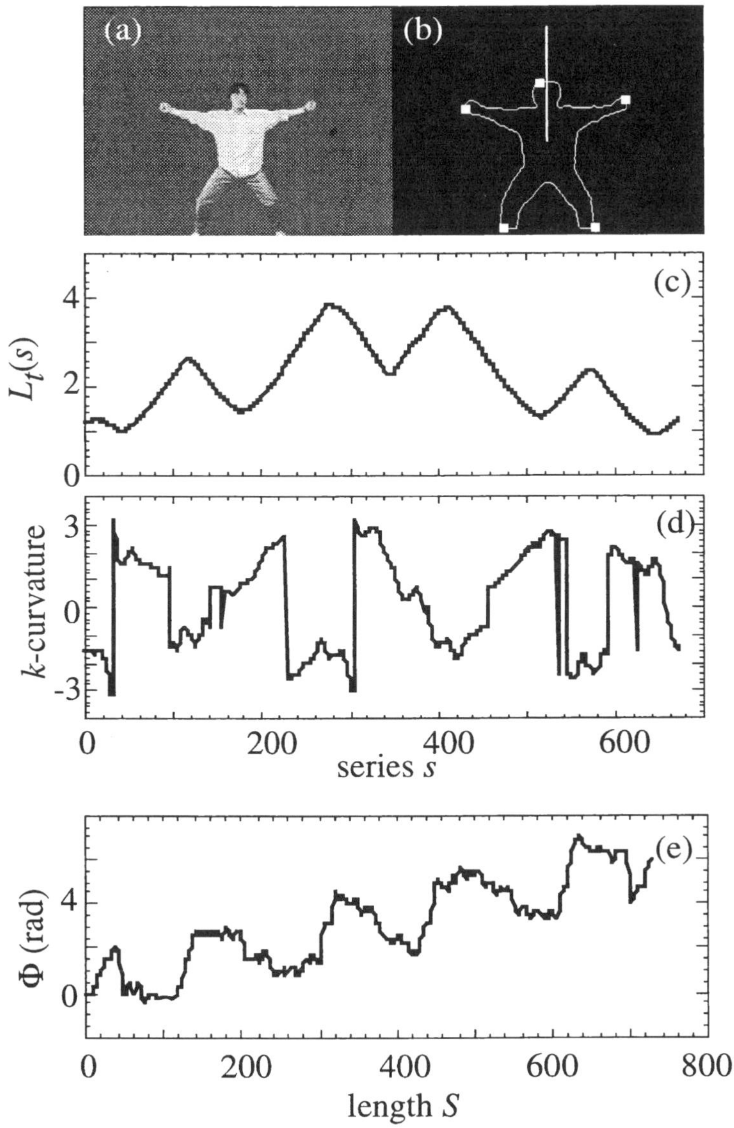

Figure 3.25. Examples of $L_t - s$ curve analysis ((a) original image, (b) contour image, (c) $L_t - s$ curve, (d) k−curvature, (e) $\Phi - S$ curve

error, which is modeled as a white noise process. By using the Kalman filter, we estimate the state vector Ξ_t as follows.

$$\hat{\Xi}_t = \hat{\Xi}_{t-1} + \boldsymbol{K}_t(\boldsymbol{\Psi}_t - \boldsymbol{\Gamma}_t\hat{\Xi}_{t-1}) \tag{3.12}$$

$$\boldsymbol{K}_t = \boldsymbol{P}_t\boldsymbol{\Gamma}_t^T\boldsymbol{R}^{-1} \tag{3.13}$$

$$\boldsymbol{P}_t = \boldsymbol{P}_{t-1} - \boldsymbol{P}_{t-1}\boldsymbol{\Gamma}_t^T(\boldsymbol{\Gamma}_t\boldsymbol{P}_{t-1}\boldsymbol{\Gamma}_t^T + \boldsymbol{R})^{-1}\boldsymbol{\Gamma}_t\boldsymbol{P}_{t-1}^T \tag{3.14}$$

where $\hat{\Xi}_t$ is the estimated vector of the state vector Ξ_t, and $\boldsymbol{K}_t$ is the Kalman gain matrix. The initial conditions are $\hat{\Xi}_0 = \boldsymbol{0}$, $\boldsymbol{P}_0 = 10^3\boldsymbol{I}$, covariance matrix $\boldsymbol{R} = \boldsymbol{I}$, where $\boldsymbol{I}$ is a unit matrix. In case of no self-occlusion, (x, y) coordniates of the significant points located by the $L_t - s$ curve analysis are used for the measurement vector $\boldsymbol{\Psi}_t$, which is required for the calculation of the Kalman filter. Note that in case of self-occlusions,$\boldsymbol{\Psi}_t$ is obtained from the results of the image difference described below. After updating the Kalman filter by inputting $\boldsymbol{\Psi}_t$ into Eq. (3.12), the optimal positions of the significant points are estimated by using Eq.(3.11). Moreover, by using Eq.(3.11) recursively, the positions of the significant points at the next frame are predicted. To minimize the computational cost and to deal with self-occlusions, a rectangular search area is placed at the predicted position for each significant point, where the coordinates of the center of the search area coincide with the predicted coordinates.

As descirbed before, $L_t - s$ curve analysis is based on silhoutte information and thus cannot locate significant points in the case of self-occlusion. Our method determines that self-occlusion has occurred if at least one of the following two conditions is satisfied: (1) no silhouette region is found, or (2) there is no local maximum in the $L_t - s$ curve. Therefore, if it turns out that self-occlusion has occurred, the location process is switched from the $L_t - s$ curve analysis to image difference. In the image difference, color data in the search area is converted to brightness data. Then, in the search area, the current frame and the previous frame are subtracted and thresholded so that movement around the significant point can be detected as a region having large brightness difference. If the search area includes such a region, a rectangle that encloses the region is calculated, and the rectangle's vertex that is closest to the predicted position is detected as the significant point. Then, the (x, y) coordinates of the vertex are used in $\boldsymbol{\Psi}_t$ for Kalman filtering.

In the image difference, if the search area does not include a region with a large brightness difference, Eq.(3.11) is recursively employed using the location results from the previous ($(t-1)$th) frame, and locating the significant point is attempted by predicting its position in the next frame. If this fails again, then if near the predicted position the $L_t - s$ curve has a local maximum, which is not tracked by another significant point, the local maximum is located as the significant point; if the $L_t - s$ curve does not have such a local maximum, the process judges that the tracking has failed for some reason (e.g. the significant point being tracked is occluded by a frontal body part) and returns to the initial calibration.

If the hand and body move simultaneously when the hand is in front of the body, it is difficult to distinguish the hand's subtraction image from the one for the body, and thus tracking the tip of the hand becomes problematic. In this case, we use the skin color information obtained from a color image to extract the hand from the subtraction image in the search area of the hand. However, color information is quite easily affected by different illuminating conditions. Therefore, we apply edge detection to the color data in the search area so as to achieve a robust estimation of the tip of the hand. Note that if the hand and/or the other significant points are occluded by the body or another body part(s), our method cannot contiue tracking.

3.4.3. 3D Reconstruction of the Significant Points

3.4.3.1 Front image. In the front image, all significant points can be estimated by the algorithm described in Section 3.4.2. Assuming a parallel projection, the coordinates of the significant points in 3D, $[X^j_{Ft}\, Y^j_{Ft}\, Z^j_{Ft}]$, are calculated by using the 2D coordinates estimated from the front image, $[x^j_t\, y^j_t]$, as follows.

$$\begin{bmatrix} X^j_{Ft} \\ Y^j_{Ft} \\ Z^j_{Ft} \end{bmatrix} = \begin{bmatrix} 1 & 0 \\ 0 & 1 \\ 0 & 0 \end{bmatrix} \begin{bmatrix} x^j_t \\ y^j_t \end{bmatrix} \tag{3.15}$$

3.4.3.2 Side image. Since it is extremely difficult to locate the tips of the hands and the tips of the feet in the silhouette for the calibration posture (Fig. 3.24(a)) in the side image, these significant points cannot be tracked. Therefore, only the top of the head is tracked by the proposed algorithm. For tracking the remaining significant points, local maxima are found by the $L_t - s$ curve analysis. The (x, y) coordinates of these local maxima are recorded and then assigned to significant points by the process of 3D reconstruction (Section 3.4.3.4). The coordinates $[x^j_t\, y^j_t]$ of the top of the head and the local maxima to be assigned to the other significant points are converted to $[X^j_{St}\, Y^j_{St}\, Z^j_{St}]$ by the following equation.

$$\begin{bmatrix} X^j_{St} \\ Y^j_{St} \\ Z^j_{St} \end{bmatrix} = \begin{bmatrix} 0 & 0 \\ 0 & 1 \\ 1 & 0 \end{bmatrix} \begin{bmatrix} x^j_t \\ y^j_t \end{bmatrix} \tag{3.16}$$

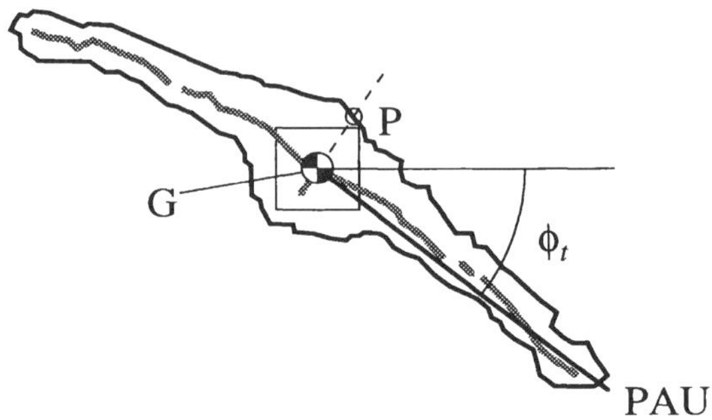

Figure 3.26. Estimating the rotation angle using the skeleton Image in the top view

3.4.3.3 Top image. The rotation angle ϕ_t of the human body is defined as the angle between the PA and x axis in the top image. Although the PAU is obtained from distance-transformed silhouette image in the case of the front and side images, the shape of the distance-transformed silhouette in the top image is normally close to a circle, and thus it is difficult to obtain the PA robustly. Therefore, as shown in Fig. 3.26, a skeleton image, instead of a distance-transformed image, is used for calculating the PA, where the PA calculation is done for the skeleton image in the small area centered at G, the center of gravity of the silhouette. As can be seen in Fig. 3.26, skeleton images can reflect the entire shape of the silhouette more reasonably than distance-transformed images so that robust estimation of the PA is possible. Note that the PA is determined so as to have a direction close to the orientation of the left hand in the calibration pose (Fig. 3.26). Point P, which is the starting point of the $L_t - s$ curve analysis, is determined as the point where the line that passes through G and which is perpendicular to the PA intersects the of $[\phi_t, \pi + \phi_t]$ region in the contour.

In the top view image, it is difficult to locate the tips of the feet in the calibration posture, becuase they are occluded by the torso. Therefore, only the tips of the hands are tracked in the top image, and the same procedure as the side image is applied to the other significant points: i.e., the local maxima in the $L_t - s$ curve analysis are assigned to the significant points by the process described in Section 3.4.3.4. The $[x_t^j \; y_t^j]$ coordinates of the tips of the hands and the located local maxima are convereted to $[X_{Tt}^j \; Y_{Tt}^j \; Z_{Tt}^j]$ by the following equation.

$$\begin{bmatrix} X_{Tt}^j \\ Y_{Tt}^j \\ Z_{Tt}^j \end{bmatrix} = \begin{bmatrix} 1 & 0 \\ 0 & 0 \\ 0 & -1 \end{bmatrix} \begin{bmatrix} x_t^j - x_t^g \\ y_t^j - y_t^g \end{bmatrix} + \begin{bmatrix} X_t^g \\ Y_t^g \\ Z_t^g \end{bmatrix} \tag{3.17}$$

where $[X_t^g \, Y_t^g \, Z_t^g]$ are the 3D coordinates of the centroid estimated from the front and side images.

3.4.3.4 Estimating 3D coordinates. The 3D coordinates $[X_t^j Y_t^j Z_t^j]$ of each significant point are estimated by combining the results obtained by using Eqs. (3.15) through (3.17). The 3D coordinates of the center of gravity and the top of the head are estimated using the results from the front and side images, as follows.

$$\begin{bmatrix} X_t^j \\ Y_t^j \\ Z_t^j \end{bmatrix} = \begin{bmatrix} X_{Ft}^j \\ (Y_{Ft}^j + Y_{St}^j)/2 \\ Z_{St}^j \end{bmatrix} \tag{3.18}$$

where $j = g, p$.

The 3D coordinates of the tips of the hands and tips of the feet are estimated using information obtained from the three view images. That is, as mentioned in Sections 3.4.3.2 and 3.4.3.3, local maxima that have not yet been assigned to significant points in the side and top images are used. Let the Y coordinate of a significant point j in the front image be denoted by Y_{Ft}^j. A candidate for j in the side image is the local maximum whose Y coordinate, Y_{St}^j, is within a small threshold distance of Y_{Ft}^j. Likewise, a local maximum in the top image is a candidate for j if its Z coordinate, Z_{Tt}^j, is within a threshold of Z_{St}^j, the Z coordinate of the candidate for j in the side image. Finally, if X_{Ft}^j, the X coordinate of j obtained for the front image, is within a threshold distance of the X coordinate of the top image's candidate for j, the top image's candidate is chosen as j. Note that if multiple candidates are obtained, the candidate whose coordinates are closest to the coordinates in the front image is determined as the located significant point. Based on the algorithm described above, the 3D coordinates of each significant point are estimated by the following equation.

$$\begin{bmatrix} X_t^j \\ Y_t^j \\ Z_t^j \end{bmatrix} = \begin{bmatrix} (X_{Ft}^j + X_{Tt}^j)/2 \\ (Y_{Ft}^j + Y_{St}^j)/2 \\ (Z_{St}^j + Z_{Tt}^j)/2 \end{bmatrix} \tag{3.19}$$

where $j = hr, hl, fr, fl$. Note that the results from the front and side images are always used to locate the centroid and the top of the head.

3.4.4. Experimental Results

3.4.4.1 Experimental System. The method in this section was coded in C++ language and implemented on a personal computer (Dual Pentium II 400MHz, Windows NT 4.0). Each of the three CCD cameras was connected to a PC, which performs 2D estimation processes such as obtaining the 2D coordinates of a significant point. The three PC's are connected to the fourth PC, which receives 2D data from the three PC's and performs 3D estimation process such as reconstructing 3D coordinates of a significant point. To simplify the image processing, green colored screens were used for the backgrounds; after extracting the silhouettes from the green backgrounds by chroma keyers in real-time in the trinocular images, each silhoutte image was digitized into a 320-by-240 pixel resolution and input into the PC. The search areas were: 30-by-30 for the tips of the hands and for the tips of the feet, and 15-by-15 for the top of the head. The order of the AR model for Kalman filtering was found by trial and error and set to $\rho = 3$ in our experiments to maintain good tracking results. The entire process for estimating human postures ran in real-time (17 frames/sec).

3.4.4.2 Experimental Results. Figures 3.27, 3.28, and 3.29 show examples of estimation results. The top of each figure shows the motion sequence from the three directions, and the bottom of the figure illustrates the 3D trajectories of the significant points estimated by the proposed method, in which the black squares and the white squares indicate the start and end positions of the trajectories, respectively. The white lines in the top of the figures, each for the end of a motion sequence, show the projections of the 3D trajectories in the individual views. As shown in these figures, the location ofthe significant points for each posture is successfully obtained, and accurate 3D reconstruction is achieved.

In Fig. 3.27, after the left hand moves in front of the torso and approaches the tip of the right hand, the left hand stretches to the left side of the body after going in front of the torso; simultaneously, the left leg also moves to the left side of the body. Self-occlusion of the left hand occurs when it crosses the silhouette of the torso; in addition, the left hand and torso move together. Despite these difficulties, it turns out that the 3D trajectory of the left hand is reconstructed correctly. In Fig. 3.28, the tip of the right foot moves above the tip of the right hand, and self-occlusion also occurs between the right hand and the right foot in the silhouette image. In Fig. 3.29, the legs cross each other. Although these postures in Figs. 3.28 and 3.29 could not be estimated by using our method based on heuristic rules described in Section 3.3, we could estimate the posture by using the method in this secion. Overall, similar tracking results were obtained for the other motions and individuals. Consequently, these results indicate the superiority of our proposed method.

In the proposed method, depending on the rotation angle ϕ_t of the body, postures that can be estimated are limited, but experimental results show the method can permit the rotation angle ϕ_t in the region of $[-\pi/4, \pi/4]$. The motions used for the experiments are smooth, but sudden changes in the Z direction can be seen in Figs. 3.28 and 3.29. The Z coordinates of the trajectory of the tip of a foot are based on the results estimated using the information from the side and top images, but since there is no tracked data for the tip of the foot in these images, the accuracy in the Z direction of the foot might be lower.

Figure 3.30 compares the left hand's trajectory estimated by the method in this section with the measurement by the magnetic sensor (Polhemus, 3SPACE FASTRAK) attached to the left hand. In Fig. 3.30, the estimated and measured 3D positions are represented by the $X - Y - Z$ coordinate, whose origin is at the tip of the left hand of the initial calibration pose. As shown in Fig. 3.30, the estimated and measured motion is as follows: the left hand is rotated to the right within a plane parallel to the $X - Z$ plane, where the elbow is stretched (arc 1 in the figure); within a plane parallel to the $X - Y$ plane, the left hand moves first downward, and then upward through its initial position to a point above the head (arc 2 through 4); finally, the left hand moves downward parallel to the $Y - Z$ plane to a point along the side of the body (arc 5). It turns out that the trajectory estimated by the method in this section coincide well with the trajectory measured by the magnetic sensor. On the other hand, if the data measured by the magnetic sensor is assumed to be true, the error (difference between the two trajectories) is approximately 20 cm on average. The difference gets large if self-occlusion occurs, and the Z direction tends to give large differences. The reasons for these are as follows: location errors in the subtraction image processing are relatively large; orthographic projection is assumed for 3D reconstruction; the camera images lack sufficient resolution, etc. Meanwhile, errors by the magnetic sensor tends to be large if the sensor gets far from the magnetic source. It can be said that the evaluation method might need more studies.

3.4.5. Summary

Section 3.4 described a real-time method for estimating body postures in 3D from trinocular images without using empirical knowledge and heuristic rules. The method in this section locates significant points of the body by applying an $L_t - s$ curve analysis to the contour of the body silhouettes extracted from the trinocular images. When self-occlusions occur in the human silhouettes, the significant points are located by using the subtraction images, which extracts a region having large brightness difference between two successive frames. Dynamic compensation is carried out by the tracking of all significant points using the AR model, whose parameters are estimated through on-line processing by the Kalman filter. The 3D coordinates of the significant points are reconstructed by using the results estimated from the three images using the geometrical relationship between the three cameras. The method in this section is implemented on a personal computer and runs in real-time (17 frames/sec).

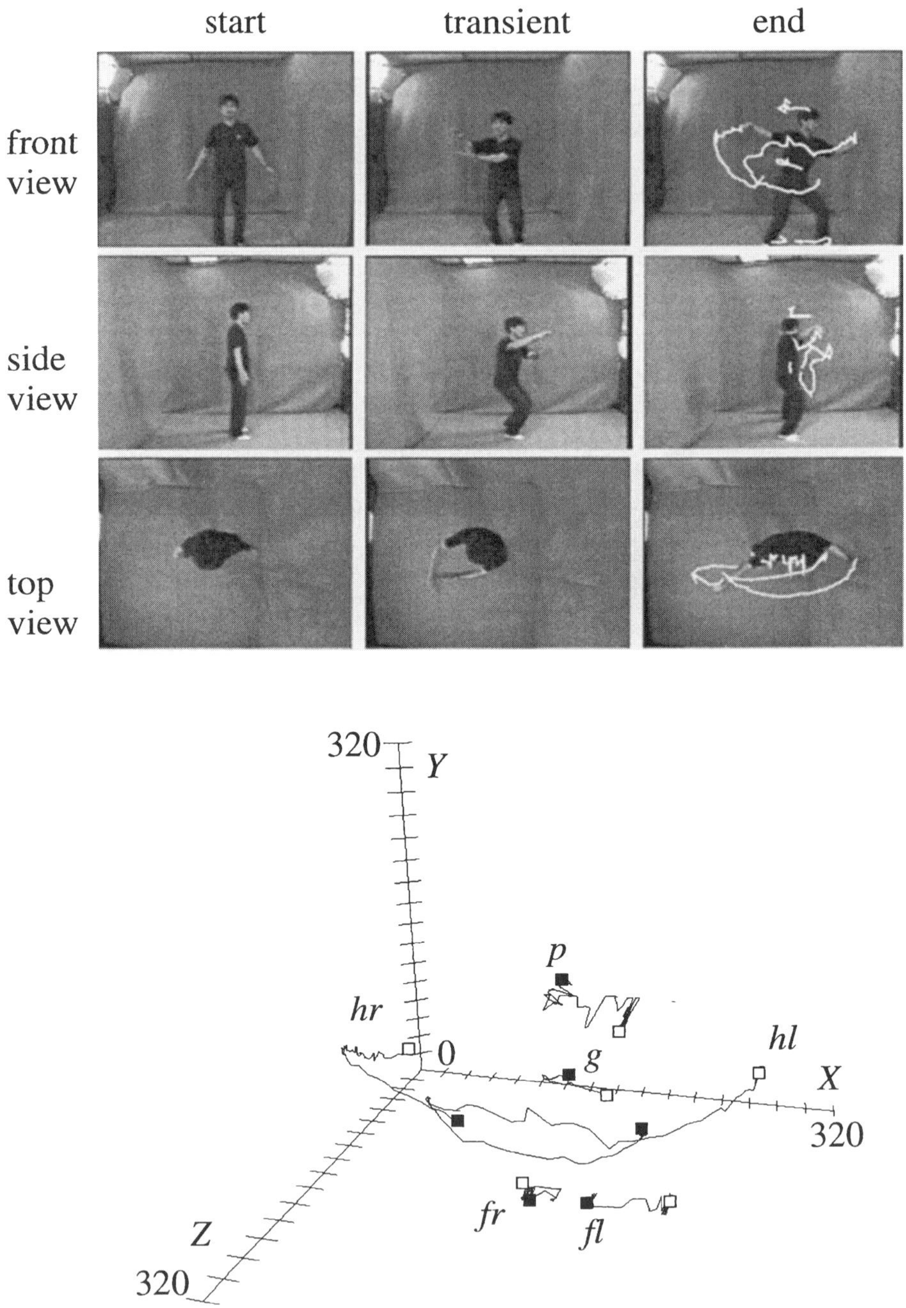

Figure 3.27. Examples of Estimating Postures in 3D

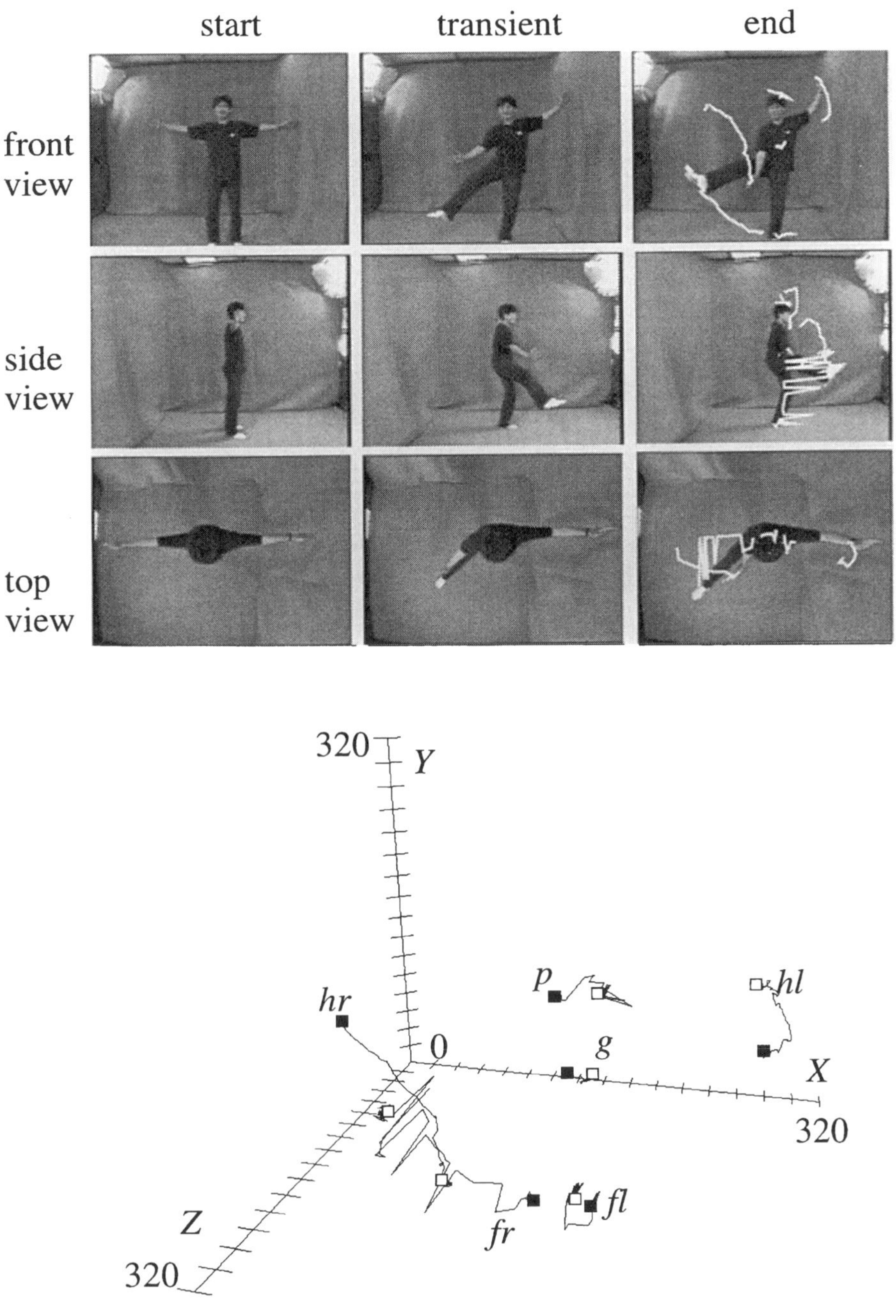

Figure 3.28. Examples of Estimating Postures in 3D

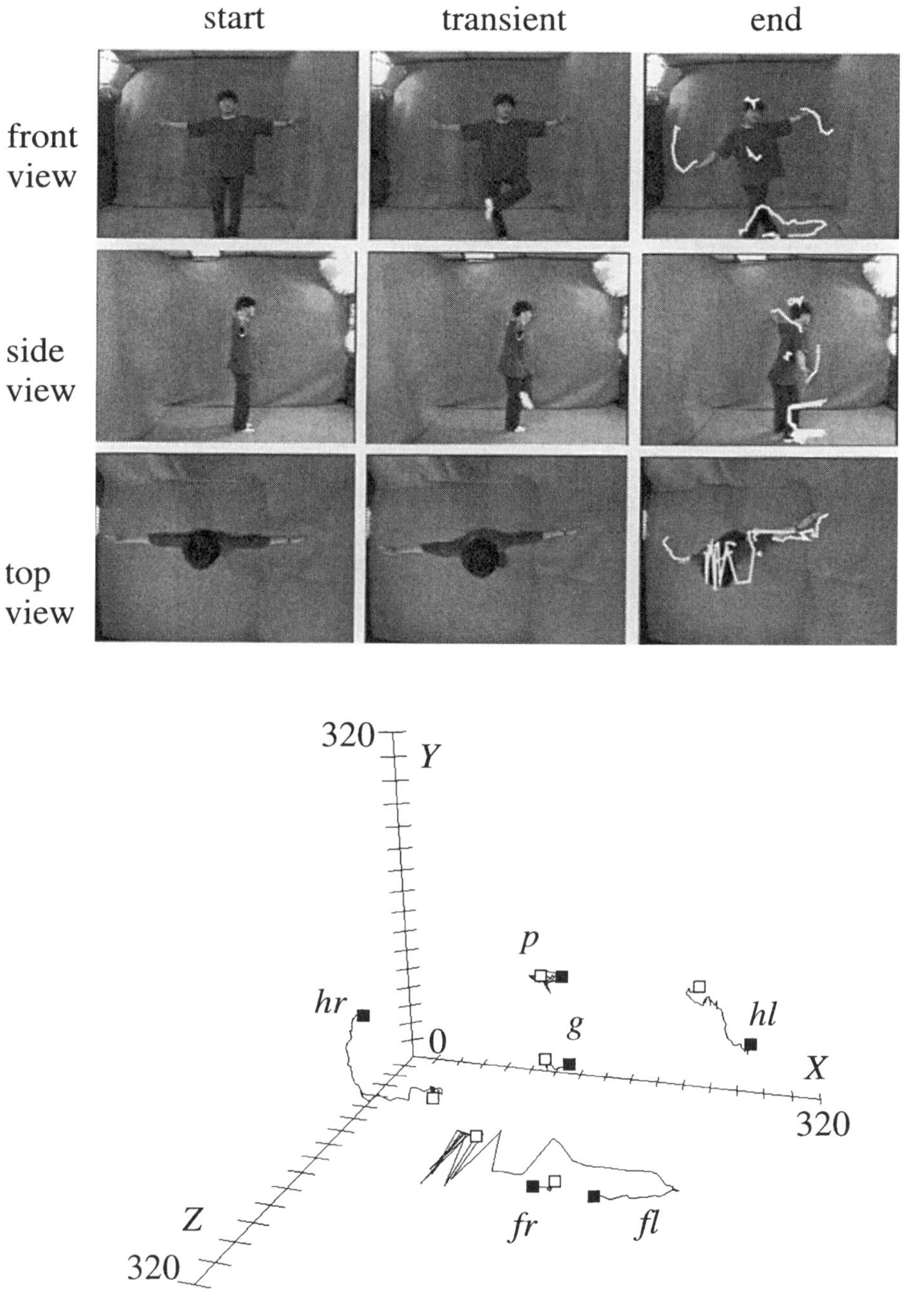

Figure 3.29. Examples of Estimating Postures in 3D

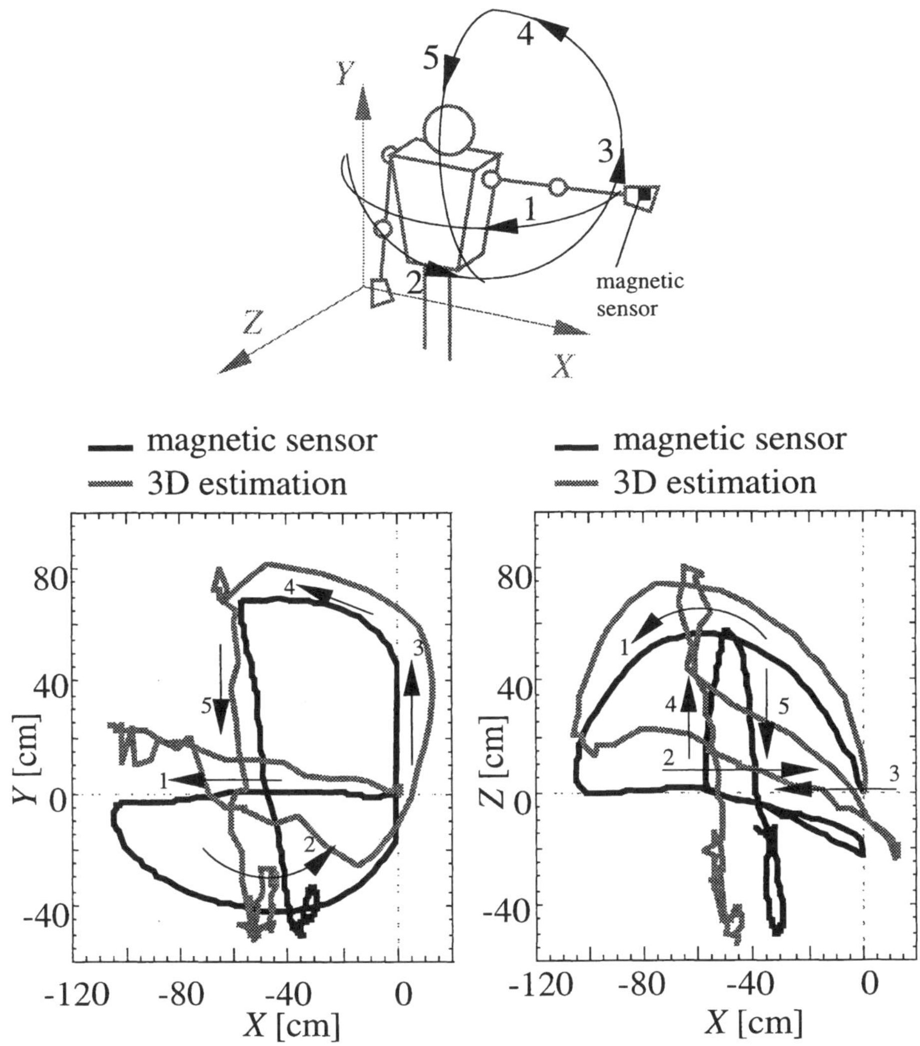

Figure 3.30. Evaluation of Estimated Positions of Left Hand

Experimental results confirm both the feasibility and the effectiveness of the method in this section.

3.5. Applications to Virtual Environments

One of the most promising and important applications of computer vision based posture estimation technologies is in the virtual environments. Motion capture systems are used for producing digital cinema and for advanced video games. But we expect such systmes will probably be replaced eventually by non-contact methods, such as technologies based on computer vision. These are off-line applications, but we believe on-line application, such as telecommunication, is another promising application area for posture estimation. This section describes our work in applications to telecommunication; more specifically, a system based on our original concept called "Virtual Metamorphosis" [Ohya et al., 1996],[Ohya et al., 1999b], which is a possible application in virtual communication environments.

3.5.1. Virtual Metamorphosis

Recently, communication between remotely located people has increased in importance due to the trend toward more collaboration and the increasing time, energy, and expenses associated with transportation. Telephones have been the major means of communication so far, but for natural human communication, not only voice but also visual information is often important. For this purpose, video phones and video conferencing systems have been developed. However, a limitation, thus far, is that users find it difficult to overcome the feeling that they are situated at distant locations. In addition, users are reluctant to have their faces appear on the receiver's display. A solution for these issues is to develop a virtual communication environment, which creates a virtual envirnment for communication by a computer connected to the network that links multiple sites.

We are aiming at realizing the above-mentioned communication environments so that remotely located people can communicate with each other via a virtual scene. Virtual metamorphosis systems are possible applications of such virtual communication environments. In the virtual metamorphosis systems, a user can change his/her form to any other form in the virtual scene. To realize a virtual metamorphosis system, the facial expressions and body postures of the user who will be "morphed" need to be estimated without physical contact in real-time and be reproduced in the form the user desires. We emphasize that facial expressions and body postures should be estimated in a non-contact fashion, more specifically, by computer vision based technologies. In conventional virtual reality systems, these estimations are carried out using contact-type methods such as attaching sensing devices to human bodies for body posture measurements, or pasting tape marks to human faces for facial deformation measurements. These alternatives give high accuracy and quick measurement, but attaching these devices is too cumbersome for most people and limits the applications of virtual metamorphosis systems.

This section illustrates two virtual metamorphosis systems we have developed. Both systems use the posture estimation methods described in earlier sections. The first virtual metamorphosis system is called the Virtual Kabuki system [Ohya et al., 1996], in which a person can be transformed to a Kabuki actor in virtual Kabuki scenes. In this system, the facial expressions and body postures of a person are estimated in real-time from the facial images acquired by the small CCD camera fixed to the helmet worn by the person and from the thermal images acquired by an infrared camera, respectively. The estimated facial expressions and body postures are then reproduced in real-time in a 3D model of a Kabuki actor on a Silicon Graphics Onyx Reality Engine II.

The second virtual metamorphosis system, called the "Shall We Dance?" system [Ebihara et al., 1998], links two sites so that two persons at two different sites can dance together in a virtual dance hall. The "Shall We Dance?" system performs facial tracking without the camera mounted helmet used in the Virtual Kabuki system, and it also estimates postures in 3D. More details on each system are described in the following.

3.5.2. Virtual Kabuki System

As shown in Fig. 3.31, the Virtual Kabuki system consists of the three main processing modules: (1) creation of 3-dimensional models of Kabuki actors, (2) real-time, passive (non-contact) estimation of facial expressions and body postures of the person, and (3) real-time reproduction of the estimated facial expressions and body postures in the Kabuki actor's model. By creating 3D models of different forms, we can change our forms to any other form.

(1) Modeling Kabuki actors

Prior to metamorphosis, the forms of the Kabuki actors need to be modeled. The 3D shapes of the Kabuki actors are represented by texture-mapped polygonal models which can be deformed to match the postures estimated by the process described in (2). The models of the Kabuki actors shown in Fig. 3.31, are rendered on a Silicon Graphics Onyx Reality Engine II.

(2) Real-time estimation of facial expressions and body postures

In conventional virtual reality systems, tape marks were pasted to the face of a user so that facial temporal deformations are measured [Ohya et al., 1995]. This method can achieve quite accurate measurements, but this is cumbersome and has limited applications. For this reason, we developed passive methods to estimate facial expressions in real-time using computer vision based tech-

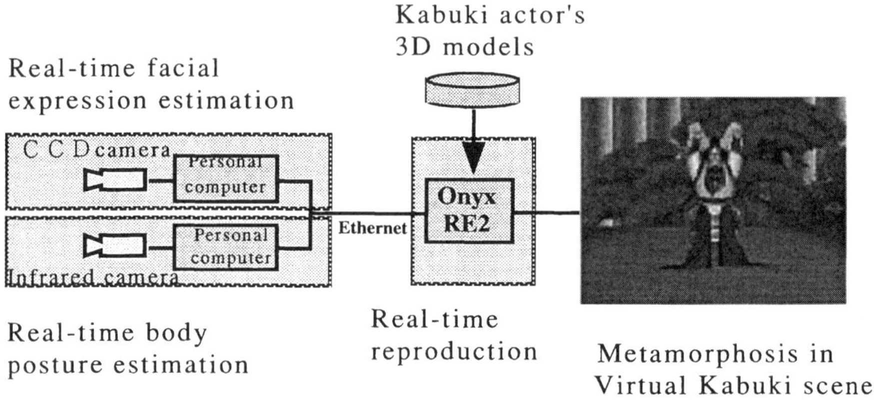

Figure 3.31. Virtual Kabuki System

niques. The posture estimation method used in the Virtual Kabuki system is described in Section 3.2.

Previous computer vision based methods classified facial expressions from a video sequence [Black et al., 1995], [Essa et al., 1995], but could not estimate facial expression at a single frame. We developed a method to estimate deformations of facial components such as the eyes and mouth using a frequency domain transform [Ebihara et al., 1996b]. The person wears a helmet to which a small CCD camera is fixed so that the camera stays at the same position relative to the face regardless of head movement. In the face image acquired by the camera, a window is applied to each facial component (Fig. 3.32), and each window is converted to frequency domain data by DCT (Discrete Cosine Transform). More specifically, each window is divided into sub-blocks, where a sub-block consists of 8 by 8 pixels. Then, DCT is applied to each sub-block, and the summations of DCT energies in the horizontal, vertical and diagonal directions in each sub-block are calculated (Fig. 3.33). A DCT feature for a direction (among the three directions) is obtained by adding the summations in that direction. Why are the DCT features useful? As the example in Fig. 3.34 illustrates, changes in the DCT features represent shape changes in the facial components. In Fig. 3.34, closing the eye decreases the value of the horizontal feature and increases the vertical feature. The DCT features for the three directions are used to reproduce the facial deformation in the face model as described below.

(3) Real-time reproduction of facial expressions and body postures

To reproduce facial expressions in the 3D model of a Kabuki actor, the DCT features estimated in (2) are utilized to deform the face model. Previously, a method for synthesizing facial expressions based on a physics model was

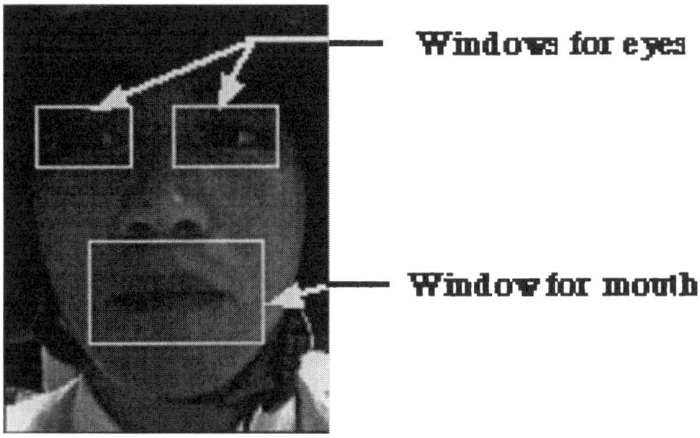

Figure 3.32. Windows for Estimating Facial Expressions

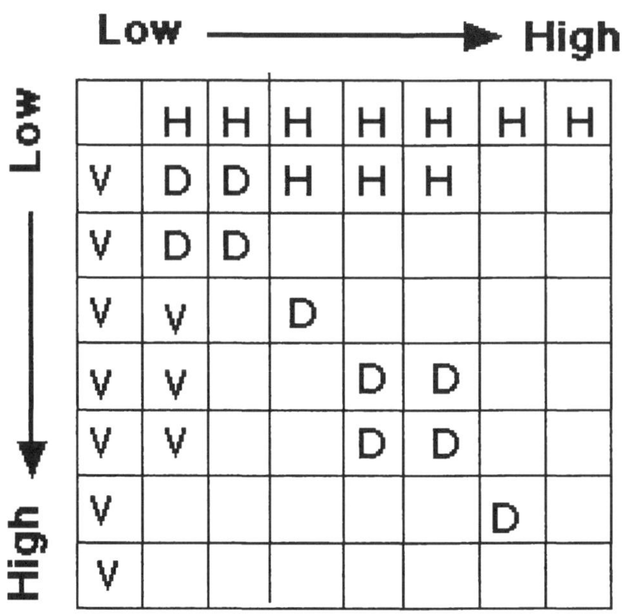

Figure 3.33. DCT Feature Calculation

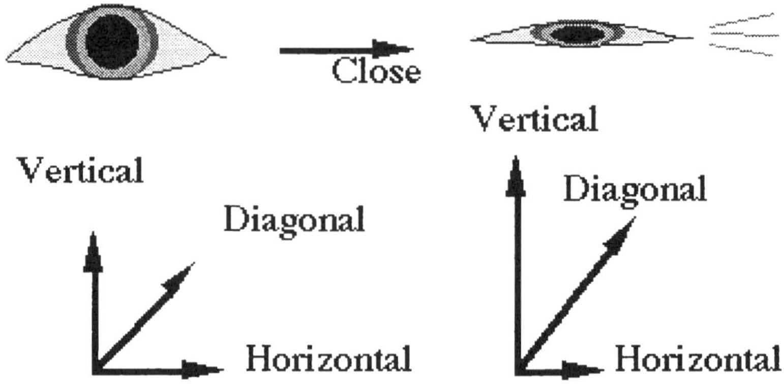

Figure 3.34. Changes in DCT Features and Facial Components' Shapes

developed [Terzopoulos et al., 1993] and showed good performance, but the system does not run in real-time. Therefore, we developed a real-time method based on anatomy for artists or plastic anatomy [Ohya et al., 1999a]. Anatomy for artists, which was proposed in Italy in the 15th century, is an artistic principle for deformation or emphasis that makes viewers feel that works (such as paintings and sculptures) are realistic.

The proposed method consists of a modeling process and reproduction process. In the modeling process, the 10 reference facial expressions chosen by the artist are generated in a 3D face model. The 3D displacement vector from a neutral facial expression is recorded at each vertex of the face model for each reference expression (Fig. 3.35). The reference expressions are chosen according to the principle of anatomy for artists; therefore, some expressions include deformations that humans cannot actually display. To generate intermediate facial expressions, the 10 reference facial expressions must be mixed. Thus, at each vertex of the 3D face model, the artist determines the mixing rate of the 3D displacement vectors of each reference facial expression for each image of a sample image set that contains many different facial expressions. Here, for the determination, the artist compares each real expression with the generated expression. Subsequently, at each vertex, a linear combination of the 10 reference displacement vectors is constructed, where each coefficient (mixing rate) of the linear combination is represented with a linear combination of the DCT features. A GA based learning procedure determines the coefficients of the linear combination of the DCT features. In the reproduction process, the DCT features obtained from the estimation process (2) are input into the linear combination for the mixing rates to calculate the displacement vector of each vertex. Figure 3.36 shows some facial expression reproductions.

To reproduce the estimated 2D body postures in a 3D model of a Kabuki actor, polynomials that convert the coordinates of the significant points from

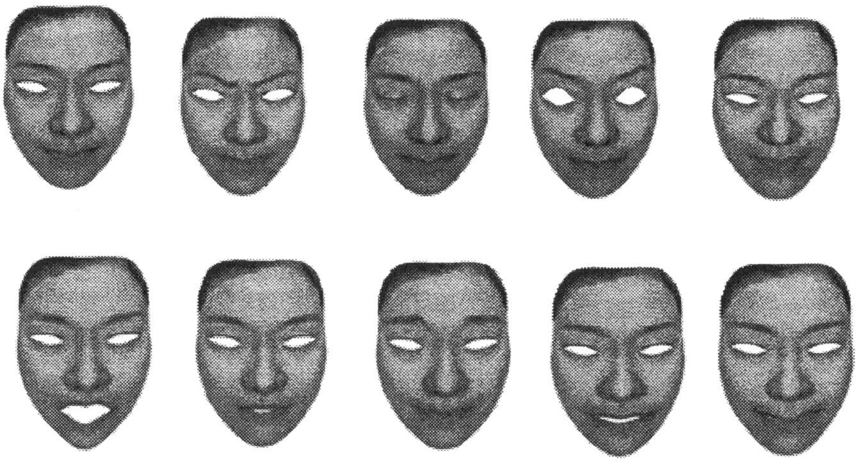

Figure 3.35. Reference Facial Expressions Created by Artist

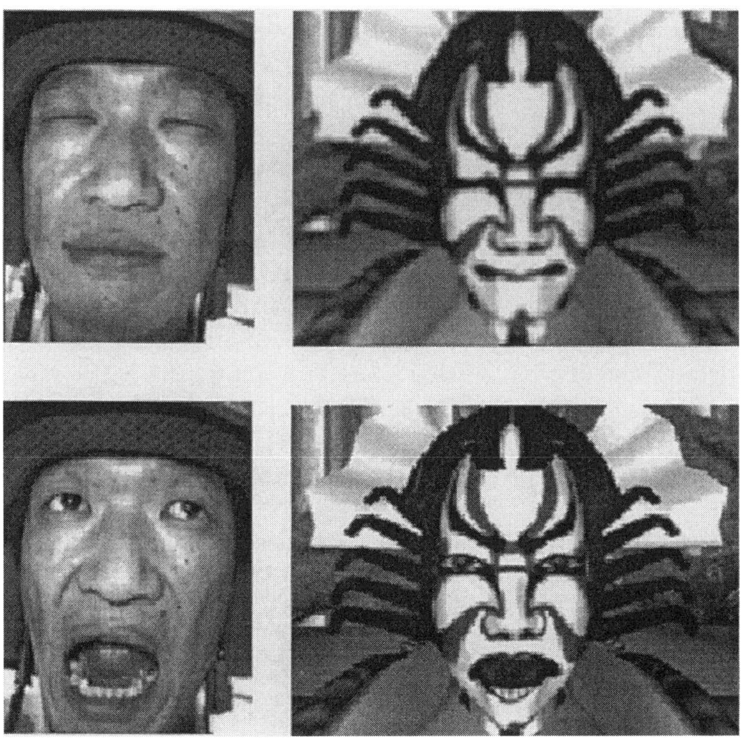

Figure 3.36. Examples of Facial Expression Reproduction

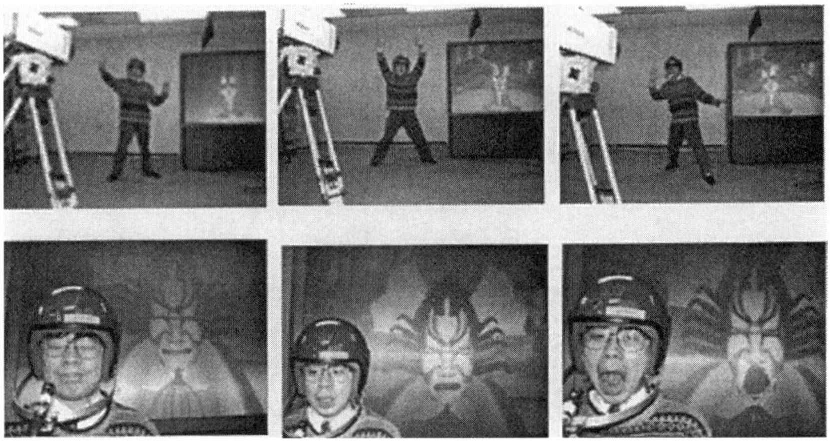

Figure 3.37. Scenes of the Virtual Kabuki System

2D to 3D are constructed in advance using a GA based learning procedure. The estimated 2D coordinates are inserted into the polynomials to reproduce 3D postures in the Kabuki actor's model in a reasonable manner. The right row of Fig. 3.10 shows the reproductions.

The estimation and reproduction processes are implemented as shown in Fig. 3.31. We use a personal computer (Gateway 2000) to estimate facial expressions. Thermal images for estimating body postures are acquired with an infrared camera (Nikon Thermal Vision LAIRD3). Human body postures are estimated from the thermal images on a Silicon Graphics Indy workstation. A Kabuki actor's 3D model and a Kabuki scene are rendered by an SGI Onyx Reality Engine 2 and displayed using a large projector screen. Some scenes of the Virtual Kabuki system are presented in Fig. 3.37. In this implementation, the process speed is approximately 20 frames/second for facial expression estimation and body posture estimation, and 12 frames/second for the rendering. The speed for the estimations is good, but the rendering speed needs improvement. We presented a live demonstration to many people at the Digital Bayou in SIGGRAPH96 [Ebihara et al., 1996a] held in New Orleans, USA, in 1996.

3.5.3. The "Shall We Dance?" system

The Virtual Kabuki system has the following limitations:

- Only one person at one site can join,
- It requires expensive facilities,

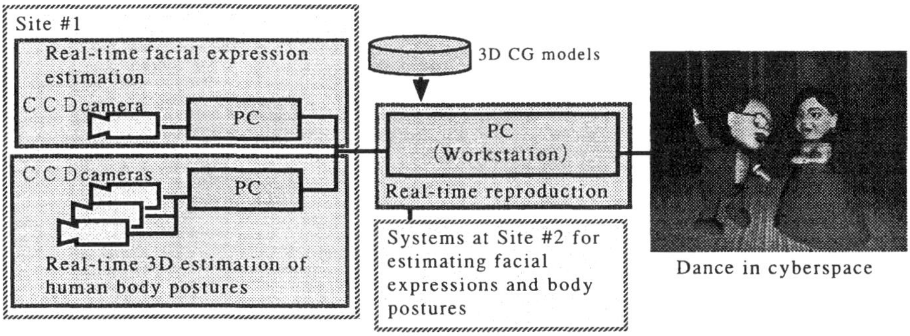

Figure 3.38. The "Shall We Dance?" system

- The person needs to wear a camera mounted helmet.

To relax these limitations, we constructed the next version of the metamorphosis systems, called the "Shall We Dance?" system. As shown in Fig. 3.38, the "Shall We Dance?" system links two sites, at each of which one person's postures and facial expression are estimtaed. The estimated data are sent to the avatar (computer graphics character) so that the estimated postures and expressions are reproduced in the avatar. Thereby, the two avatars are controlled by the two persons at the two sites; that is, the two persons can dance together in the virtual dance hall.

The camera mounted helmet worn by the participant in the Virtual Kabuki system was replaced with a camera separated from the person. For the DCT based estimation of deformations of facial components, the face should ideally be observed continually from the front. Therefore, our system uses a gaze controllable camera whose viewing direction can be computer controlled. Specifically, we use the SONY EVI-30, which can be panned and tilted by a personal computer. The camera automatically tracks the face of participant, whose facial expressions can be estimated in the same manner as that of the helmet method. In the tracking method, the facial skin color and geometrical relationship between facial components are learned in advance, and these data are used to control the camera so that the centroid of the skin color area stays at the center of each frame. Then, windows are applied to the facial components using the geometrical relationship so that deformations of facial components can be estimated with the DCT based approach. Figure 3.39 shows a face tracking and window application.

In the "Shall We Dance?" system, the person's postures are estimated in 3D by using the method described in Section 3.4. The system was implemented on personal computers as described in Section 3.4, and runs at approximately 12 frames/second, which is quite good for human-to-human communication. "Shall We Dance?" was demonstrated in many places, including

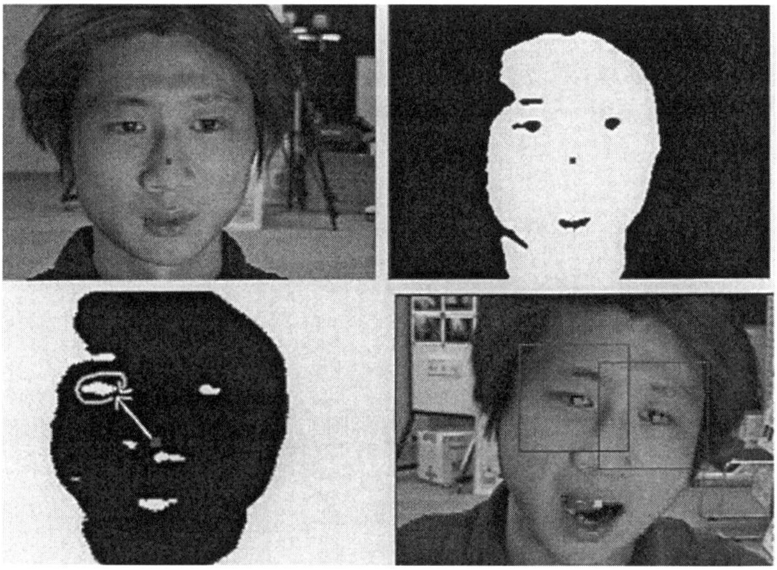

Figure 3.39. Automatic Face Tracking

SIGGRAPH98 [Ebihara et al., 1998], and the effectiveness and robustness of the system were confirmed.

3.6. Discussion and Conclusion

This chapter described posture estimation methods that can locate the positions of significant points of the human body, such as the top of the head and the tips of hands and feet, in real-time using approaches based on computer vision. We developed three systems successively. The second and third are based on the first and second, respectively. The three systems described in this chapter can be summarized in the order their development as follows.

1 The first system locates significant points on the body by analyzing the contour of the human silhouette extracted from the background in a monocular thermal image. To analyze the contour, empirical knowledge about human body shapes and heuristic rules are utilized. The positions of the elbows and knees, which are in general difficult to locate by the contour analysis method, are estimated using a learning procedure based on a genetic algorithm. The prototype system works in a robust and stable manner at real-time rate, despite difficult lighting and background conditions, but the posture estimation is only in 2D.

2 For a 3D posture estimation, the second system uses three color CCD cameras that observe a person from three directions: front, side, and top.

Using a uniform colored background, human silhouettes are extracted from the three images. The location algorithm used in the first system is applied to the front and side images. A diffferent algorithm that can also estimate the rotation angle of the body (orientation of the torso) is applied to the top image. Next, the 3D coordinates of each significant point are obtained from the two selected views. The views are selected by evaluating the appropriateness of the three views, where the appropriateness could indicate the probabily of occlusion. The prototype system shows good performance, but it is difficult to deal with the postures that cause self-occlusions. In addition, the empirical knowledge and heuristic rules cause the lack of generality of posture estimation: i.e, arbitrary postures cannot be treated.

3 To avoid using the empirical knowledge and heuristic rules, the third system locates significant points of the human body by applying a function based curve analysis to the contour of a human silhouette in the trinocular images. When self-occlusions occur in the human silhouettes, the significant points are located by using the subtraction images, which extracts a region having large a brightness difference between two successive frames. Dynamic compensation is carried out by the tracking of all significant points using the AR model, whose parameters are estimated through on-line processing by the Kalman filter. The 3D coordinates of the significant points are reconstructed by using the results estimated from the three images using the geometrical relationship between the three cameras. After observing the initial calibration pose, the third system can keep estimating the person's postures in 3D.

As an application of the posture estimation methods summarized above, they are successfully applied to the virtual metamorphosis systems. In these applications, the estimated postures of users are reproduced in avatars (computer graphics characters) in virtual environments. This allows one to feel as if he or she changes his or her form to the other representations in the virtual settings.

However, real-time estimation of postures in 3D is not completely solved. Remaining issues are listed in the following.

- Our system cannot track a significant point that is occluded by another body part. One idea for solving this problem is to increase the number of cameras so as to minimize the probability of occlusions, but this might cause huge computation costs.

- More robust tracking algorithm is needed for self-occlusion cases. More useful method for utilizing color information should be developed.

References

Azarbayejani, A., Wren, C., and Pentland, A. (1996). Real-Time 3-D Tracking of the Human Body. In *Proc. of IMAGE'COM 96*.

Black, M.J. et al. (1995). Tracking and recognizing rigid and nonrigid facial motions using local parametric models of image motion. In *Proc. Fifth International Conference on Computer Vision*, pages 374–381.

Chen, Z. and Lee, H. (1992). Knowledge-guided visual perception of 3-D human gait from a single image sequence. *IEEE Trans. on SMC*, 22(2):336–342.

Ebihara, K., Kurumisawa, J., Ohya, J., Kishino, F., and Nakatsu, R. (1996a). Virtual Kabuki System. In *SIGGRAPH 96 Visual Proceedings*, page 87.

Ebihara, K., Ohya, J. and Kishino, F. (1996b). Real-time facial expression detection based on frequency domain transform. In *Proc. of Visual Communications and Image Processing '96, SPIE*, 2727:916-926.

Ebihara, K., Kurumisawa, J., Sakaguchi, T., Ohya, J., Davis, L.S., Horprasert, T., Haritaoglu, R.I., Pentland, A., and Wren, C. (1998). Shall We Dance?. In *ACM SIGGRAPH98, Enhanced Realities, Conference Abstracts and Applications*, page 124.

Essa, L.A., et al. (1995). Facial expression recognition using a dynamic model and motion energy. In *Proc. Fifth International Conference on Computer Vision*, pages 360–367.

Gavrila, D.M., and Davis, L.S. (1996). 3-D model-based tracking of humans in action: a multi-view approach. In *Proc. of IEEE Computer Society Conference on Computer Vision and Pattern Recognition'96*, pages 73–80.

D. E. Goldberg, D.E. (1989). *Genetic Algorithm in search, optimization, and machine learning*, Addison-Wesley.

Haritaoglu, Harwood, I.D., and Davis, L.S. (1998). W4: Who? When? Where? What? A Real Time System for Detecting and Tracking People. In *Proc. of Third IEEE International Conference on Automatic Face and Gesture Recognition*, pages 222–227.

Horprasert, T., Haritaoglu, I., Wren, C., Harwood, D., Davis, L., and Pentland, A. (1998). Real-time 3D Motion Capture. In *Proc. of 1998 Workshop on Perceptual User Interfaces (PUI'98), San Francisco, Calif.*, pages 87–90.

Iwasawa S., Ebihara K., Ohya J., and Morishima S. (1997). Real-time estimation of human body posture from monocular thermal images. In *Proc. of 1997 IEEE Computer Society Conference on Computer Vision and Pattern Recognition*, pages 15–20.

Iwasawa S., Ohya J., Takahashi K., Sakaguchi T., Ebihara K., and Morishima S. (2000). Human body postures from trinocular camera images. In *Proc. of Fourth IEEE International Conference on Automatic Face and Gesture Recognition*, pages 326–331.

Kameda, Y., Minoh, M., and Ikeda, K. (1993). Three dimensional pose estimation of an articulated object from its silhouette image. In *Proc. of Asian Conference on Computer Vision*, pages 612–615.

Kurakake, S. and Nevatia, R. (1992). Description and tracking of moving articulated objects. In *Proc. of 11th International Conference on Pattern Recognition*, I:491–495.

Ohya, J. and Kishino, F. (1994). Human Posture Estimation from Multiple Images Using Genetic Algorithm. In *Proc. of 12th International Conference on Pattern Recognition*, pages 750–753.

Ohya, J., Kitamura, Y., Takemura, H., Ishii, H., Kishino, F., and Terashima, N. (1995). Virtual Space Teleconferencing: Real-time reproduction of 3D human images. *Journal of Visual Communication and Image Representation*, 6(1):1-25.

Ohya, J., Ebihara, K., Kurumisawa J., and Nakatsu, R. (1996). Virtual Kabuki Theater: Towards the Realization of Human Metamorphosis Systems. In *Proc. of 5th IEEE International Workshop on Robot and Human Communication*, pages 416–421.

Ohya, J., Ebihara, K., and Kurumisawa, J. (1999a). Artistic anatomy based, real-time reproduction of facial expressions in 3D face models. In *Proc. of IEEE International Conference on Multimedia Systems and Computing*, 2:684–689.

Ohya, J., Ebihara, K., Kurumisawa, J., Iwasawa, S., Nakatsu, R., Harwood, D., and Horprasert, T. (1999b). Virtual Metamorphosis. *IEEE Multimedia*, 6(2):29–39.

Pentland, A. (1990). Automatic extraction of deformable part models. *International Journal of Computer Vision*, 4:107–126.

Pentland, A. and Sclaroff, S. (1991a). Closed-form solutions for physically based shape modeling and recognition. *IEEE Trans. on Pattern Analysis and Machine Intelligence*, 13(7):715–129.

Pentland, A. and Horowitz, B. (1991b). Recovery of nonrigid motion and structure. *IEEE Trans. on Pattern Analysis and Machine Intelligence*, 13(7):730–742.

K. Rohr, K. (1993). Incremental recognition of pedestrians from image sequences. In *Proc. of IEEE Computer Society Conference on Computer Vision and Pattern Recognition*, pages 8–13.

Takahashi K., Sakaguchi T., and Ohya J. (2000). Remarks on a real-time 3D human body posture estimation method using trinocular images. In *Proc. of 15th International Conference on Pattern Recognition*, 4:693–697.

Terzopoulos, D. and Metaxas, D. (1991). Dynamic 3D models with local and global deformations: deformable superquadrics. *IEEE Trans. on Pattern Analysis and Machine Intelligence*, 13(7):703–714.

Terzopoulos, D. and Waters, K. (1993). Analysis and synthesis of facial image sequences using physical and anatomical models. *IEEE Transactions on Pattern Analysis and Machine Intelligence*, 15(6):569–579.

Wren, C., Azarbayejani, A., Darrel, T., and Pentland, A. (1996). Pfinder: Real-Time Tracking of the Human Body. In *Proc. of the 2nd International Conference on Automatic Face and Gesture Recognition*, pages 51–56.

Yamamoto, M., Ohta, Y., Yamagiwa, T., Yagishita, K., Yamanaka, H., and Ohkubo, N. (2000). Human Action Tracking Guided by Key-Frame. In *Proc. of Fourth IEEE International Conference on Automatic Face and Gesture Recognition*, pages 354–361.

Chapter 4

RECOGNIZING HUMAN BEHAVIOR USING HIDDEN MARKOV MODELS

Junji Yamato
Nippon Telegraph and Telephone Corporation.
R&D strategy department.
2-3-1 Otemachi, Chiyoda-ku, Tokyo 100-8116, Japan

Abstract This chapter describes a new human behavior recognition method based on Hidden Markov Models (HMM). We use a feature-based bottom-up approach using HMM, which can provide a learning capability and time-scale invariability. To apply HMM to our aim, time-sequential images are transformed to an image feature vector sequence, and the sequence is converted to a symbol sequence by Vector Quantization. In learning human behavior categories, the model parameters of HMM are optimized so as to best describe training sequences. For recognition, the model that best matches the observed sequence is chosen. A new VQ method and HMM configuration for behavior recognition is proposed and evaluated. Experimental results of real time-sequential images of sports scenes show a higher than 90% recognition rate. We also describe an example application of this behavior recognition method to content-based video database retrieval.

Keywords: Behavior recognition, Hidden Markov Models, Vector quantization, content-based image retrieval

4.1. Background and overview

In recent years, motion related topics have been major concerns in computer vision. Among moving objects in real scenes, human beings are critical targets for recognition tasks because human behavior recognition algorithms can greatly contribute to the realization of automatic monitoring systems for various important applications. This chapter introduces a new algorithm for recognizing human behavior from time-sequential images, where an observed human behavior is classified as belonging to one of the human behavior categories.

Existing approaches related to human behavior recognition include the top-down methods based on geometric body reconstruction [Horowitz and Pentland, 1991; O'Rouke and Badler, 1980; Yamamoto, 1991] and bottom-up methods based on low-level image features.

Most systems based on the top-down approach employ a geometrical model of the human body, where human body parts are described as cylinders [Hogg, 1983], super quadrics [Horowitz and Pentland, 1991], and so on. Using spatio-temporal analysis [Yamamoto, 1991], constraint propagations[O'Rouke and Badler, 1980] or modal analysis [Horowitz and Pentland, 1991], geometric model parameters are determined from images. Accordingly, the posture of a human is extracted from the image and the representation obtained. A series of model parameters are obtained from a series of images.

In the above 'model-based' top-down approaches, the reconstruction of the human body shape yields rich and useful representations such as joint angle parameters if the reconstruction is successful. However, the reconstruction procedures are neither robust nor reliable for real images because they are usually not clear enough to automatically fit the models or to extract the high-level representations needed. Therefore, although pattern classification techniques can be used to recognize a series of model parameters extracted from image sequences, hardly any results for human bahavior recognition by the model-based approach have been reported. Improving the robustness of reconstruction is important in this type of approach because failure in the reconstruction stage causes fatal errors for the subsequent recognition procedure. However, as the qualitative vision paradigm [Aloimonos, 1990] points out, is reconstruction really necessary for human behavior recognition? Our purpose is to recognize human behavior from time-sequential images, not to obtain geometric representations of human bodies. However, as described above, many recent motion related research works have focused on reconstruction of motion parameters of rigid or non-rigid moving objects [Terzopoulos and Metaxas, 1991]. Since we focus on recognition, we do not pursue reconstruction because the representation obtained by geometric reconstruction is not actually needed. Instead, we utilize low-level image features in a bottom-up way.

Bottom up approaches that heuristically utilize low-level features obtained from real images have been the subject of various studies. In these approaches, low-level image features, such as the areas of human candidate regions, are used for counting the number of pedestrians in real scenes. In general, low-level features do not provide descriptions as rich as those of model based representation but are more robust than model fitting procedures.

We emphasize the robustness of the bottom-up approach, but conventional works have succeeded only in primitive applications such as detecting movements or counting the number of people. Another problem with bottom-up approaches is that describing behavior categories in a low-level representation is more difficult than in a high-level (model-based) representation. This is because relations between dimensions of the feature vector and the high-level description of a category are not explicit. Furthermore, the dimension of the feature vector is usually too large to be understood intuitively.

Therefore, in bottom-up approaches, how can we enable the system to recognize more complicated actions? How can we describe the definition of categories without model-based high-level representation?

To solve these issues, it would be effective to develop a learning procedure that uses low-level image features.

Our problem is to classify observed low-level image feature sequences into human behavior categories. Usually, this kind of problem is formalized as a supervised learning problem in the pattern classification field. Unlike most classical pattern classification techniques, the data to be classified is time-sequential data.

To achieve a learning capability for time-sequential image data, we employ the Hidden Markov Models (HMM) [Huang et al., 1990], which can deal with time-sequential data and can provide time-scale invariability as well as learning capability for recognition. Although HMMs have been successfully used in speech recognition, they have been applied to only a few problems in the computer vision field: planar shape classification [He and Kundu, 1991; Mao and Kung, 1990], handwritten word recognition [Kunda et al., 1989], face image segmentation and recognition [Samaria and Fallside, 1993; Samaria, 1993], and modeling of eye movement [Rimey and Brown, 1990], however, HMMs have never been applied to behavior recognition before.

In our proposed approach based on HMM, time-sequential images of human behavior are transformed to an image feature vector sequence by extracting a feature vector from each image of the time-sequential images[Yamato et al., 1992]. In our current implementation, the mesh feature[Umeda, 1982] is used for the low-level image feature. Then, each feature vector of the sequence is assigned a symbol that corresponds to a codeword in the codebook created by Vector Quantization [Huang et al., 1990] applied to the feature vectors of the sample data set for training. Consequently, the time-sequential images are converted to a symbol sequence. In the learning phase, the model parameters of each HMM are optimized so as to best describe the training symbol sequences for each category of human behavior to be recognized. For human behavior recognition, the model that best matches the observed symbol sequence is chosen as the recognized category.

In the following, section 4.2 gives more details on the HMM and its recognition and learning procedures. Section 4.3 illustrates how time-sequential images are converted to a symbol sequence that the HMMs can deal with. Section 4.4 gives experimental results of behavior recognition using tennis action scenes. We discuss the improvement of VQ in section 4.5. Finally, section 4.6 describes an application of this method to content-based video database retrieval.

4.2. Hidden Markov Models

4.2.1. Outline

HMM, which has recently been applied with particular success to speech recognition, is a kind of stochastic state transition model [Rabiner and Juang, 1986]. HMM makes it possible to deal with time-sequential data and can provide time-scale invariability in recognition. Moreover, HMM is characterized by its learning ability, which is achieved by presenting time-sequential data to the HMM and automatically optimizing the model with the data.

In HMM there are states, and a probability of transition is assigned from one state to another. As time goes, state transitions occur stochastically. Like Markov models, states at any time depend only on the state at the preceding time, but in HMM a symbol is yielded from one of the states according to the probabilities assigned to the states. HMM's states are not directly observable, and can be observed only through a sequence of observed symbols. To describe a discrete HMM[1] , the following notations are defined.

$T =$ length of observation sequence.
$Q = \{q_i, q_2, \ldots, q_N\}$: set of states.
$N =$ number of states in the model.
$V = \{v_1, v_2, \ldots, v_M\}$: set of possible output symbols.
$M =$number of observation symbols.
$\mathbf{A} = \{a_{ij} | a_{ij} = \Pr(s_{t+1} = q_j | s_t = q_i)\}$: state transition probability, where:
a_{ij} is the probability of transiting from state q_i to state q_j.
$\mathbf{B} = \{b_j(k) | b_j(k) = \Pr(v_k | s_t = q_j)\}$: symbol output probability, where:
$b_j(k)$ is the probability of output symbol v_k at state q_j.
$\pi = \{\pi_i | \pi_i = \Pr(s_1 = q_i)\}$: initial state probability.
$\lambda = \{\mathbf{A}, \mathbf{B}, \pi\}$: complete parameter set of the model.
Using this model, transitions are described as follows:

$S = \{s_t\},\ t = 1, 2, \ldots, T$: state s_t is the t th state (non-observable)
$O = O_1, O_2, ..., O_T$: observed symbol sequence (length=T)

Figure 4.1 shows the concept of the HMM with a transition graph. There are four states in this example, which are indicated as circles. Each directed line is a transition from one state to another, where the transition probability is indicated by the character alongside the line.

For example, if the HMM is in state q_1 at time t, there is a probability of a_{12} that its next state at time $t+1$ will be q_2. Accordingly, the HMM has N states, the state transition probability of a_{ij} makes an $N \times N$ matrix. Note that there

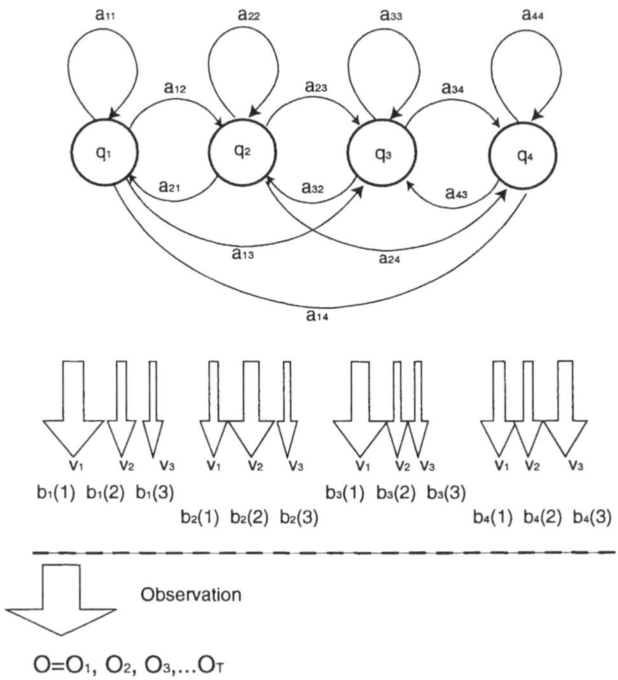

Figure 4.1. Concept of Hidden Markov Models

are also the transition paths from states to themselves. These paths can provide the HMM with time-scale invariability because they allow the HMM to stay at the same state for any duration.

Each state of the HMM stochastically outputs a symbol. In state q_j, symbol v_k is output with a probability of $b_j(k)$. If there are M kinds of symbols, $b_j(k)$ becomes an $N \times M$ matrix. HMM outputs a symbol sequence $O = O_1, O_2, \ldots, O_T$ from time 1 to T. We can observe the symbol sequences output from the HMM, but we cannot observe the HMM states. The initial state of the HMM is also determined stochastically by the initial state probability π. Each HMM is characterized by three matrices: state transition probability matrix $\mathbf{A}$, symbol output probability matrix $\mathbf{B}$, and initial state probability matrix π.

The parameters of $\mathbf{A}, \mathbf{B}$, and π are determined by the learning procedure described in 4.2.3. As described in 4.2.2, an HMM is created for each category to be recognized. Recognizing time-sequential symbols involves classifying which HMM produced the observed symbol sequence. The recognition and learning procedures are explained in 4.2.2 and 4.2.3.

4.2.2. Recognition

To recognize observed symbol sequences, we create one HMM for each category. For a classifier of C categories, we choose the model that best matches the observations from C HMMs $\lambda_i = \{\mathbf{A}_i, \mathbf{B}_i, \pi_i\}, i = 1 \ldots C$. This means that when a sequence of an unknown category is given, we calculate $\Pr(\lambda_i|O)$ for each HMM λ_i and select λ_{c^*}, where

$$c^* = \arg\max_i(\Pr(\lambda_i|O)) \tag{4.1}$$

Given the observation sequence $O = O_1, \ldots O_T$ and the HMM λ_i, according to the Bayes rule, the problem is how to evaluate $\Pr(O|\lambda_i)$, which is the probability that the sequence was generated by the HMM λ_i. This probability is calculated by using the 'forward algorithm' [Huang et al., 1990].

The forward algorithm is defined as follows:

Define:

$$\alpha_t(i) \equiv \Pr(O_1, O_2, \ldots, O_t, s_t = q_i|\lambda). \tag{4.2}$$

$\alpha_t(i)$ is called the forward variable and can be calculated recursively as follows:

$$\alpha_t(j) = \{\sum_i \alpha_{t-1}(i)a_{ij}\}b_j(O_t) \tag{4.3}$$

$$\alpha_1 = \pi_i b_i(O_1) \tag{4.4}$$

Then

$$\Pr(O|\lambda) = \sum_{i \in S_F} \alpha_T(i)\lambda_{c^*}, c^* = \arg\max_i(\Pr(\lambda_i|O)) \tag{4.5}$$

We can calculate the likelihood of each HMM by using the above equation and select the most likely HMM as the recognition result. Since the likelihood is calculated from the entire length of the pattern as described above, the time scale variance, time shift and failure in vector quantization have little influence on the accuracy of the likelihood. Consequently, the advantage of HMMs for time-sequential pattern recognition is its robustness to time scale variance and shift.

4.2.3. Learning

In the learning phase, each HMM must be trained so that it is most likely to generate the symbol patterns for its category. Training an HMM involves optimizing the model parameters (A, B, π) to maximize the probability of the observation sequence $\Pr(O|\lambda)$. The Baum-Welch algorithm is used for these estimations.

Define:

$$\beta_t(i) \equiv P(O_{t+1}, \ldots, O_T|s_t = q_i, \lambda) \tag{4.6}$$

$\beta_t(i)$ is called the backward variable and can also be solved inductively in a manner similar to the forward variable $\alpha_t(i)$.

$$\gamma_t(i) \equiv P(s_t = q_i | O_1, O_2, \ldots, O_T, \lambda) \tag{4.7}$$
$$= \frac{P(s_t = q_i, O_1, O_2, \ldots, O_T | \lambda)}{P(O_1, O_2, \ldots, O_T | \lambda)}$$
$$= \frac{\alpha_t(i)\beta_t(i)}{P(O|\lambda)}. \tag{4.8}$$

$$\xi_t(i,j) \equiv P(s_t = q_i, s_{t+1} = q_j | O_1, O_2, \ldots, O_T, \lambda) \tag{4.9}$$
$$= \frac{P(s_t = q_i, s_{t+1} = q_j, O_1, O_2, \ldots, O_T | \lambda)}{P(O_1, O_2, \ldots, O_T | \lambda)}$$
$$= \frac{\alpha_t(i) a_{ij} b_j(O_{t+1}) \beta_{t+1}(j)}{P(O|\lambda)}. \tag{4.10}$$

Using these equations, HMM parameters λ can be improved to $\tilde{\lambda}$. The re-estimation equations from $\lambda = (A, B, \pi)$ to $\tilde{\lambda} = (\tilde{A}, \tilde{B}, \tilde{\pi})$ are:

$$\tilde{a}_{ij} = \frac{\sum_{t=1}^{T-1} \xi_t(i,j)}{\sum_{t=1}^{T-1} \gamma_t(i)}; \tag{4.11}$$
$$\tilde{b}_i(k) = \frac{\sum_{t \in \{t | O_t = v_k\}} \gamma_t(i)}{\sum_{t=1} T \gamma_t(i)}; \tag{4.12}$$
$$\tilde{\pi}_i = \gamma_1(i). \tag{4.13}$$

This learning converges if $\tilde{\lambda} = \lambda$. The Baum-Welch algorithm does not always find the global maximum, but it does find the local maximum of $\Pr(O|\lambda)$.

4.3. Applying HMM to time-sequential images

To apply HMM to time-sequential images $I = \{I_1, I_2, \ldots I_T\}$, the images must be transformed to symbol sequences O (Figure 4.2) in the learning and recognition phases. From each frame of images sequence I_i , a feature vector $f_i \in R^n$ ($i = 1, 2, \ldots, T, n$ is the dimension of the feature vector) is extracted, and f_i is assigned to the symbol v_j chosen from the symbol set V.

It is necessary to associate the symbol set V with the feature space R^n. For this, the feature space is divided into clusters by a pattern classification technique, and the symbols are assigned to the clusters. We used vector quantization [Huang et al., 1990] here, as is usual in HMM applications. Vector quantization requires codewords $g_j \in R^n$, which represent the centers of the clusters in the feature R^n space. Codeword g_j is assigned to symbol v_j . Consequently, the size of the code book equals the number of HMM output symbols.

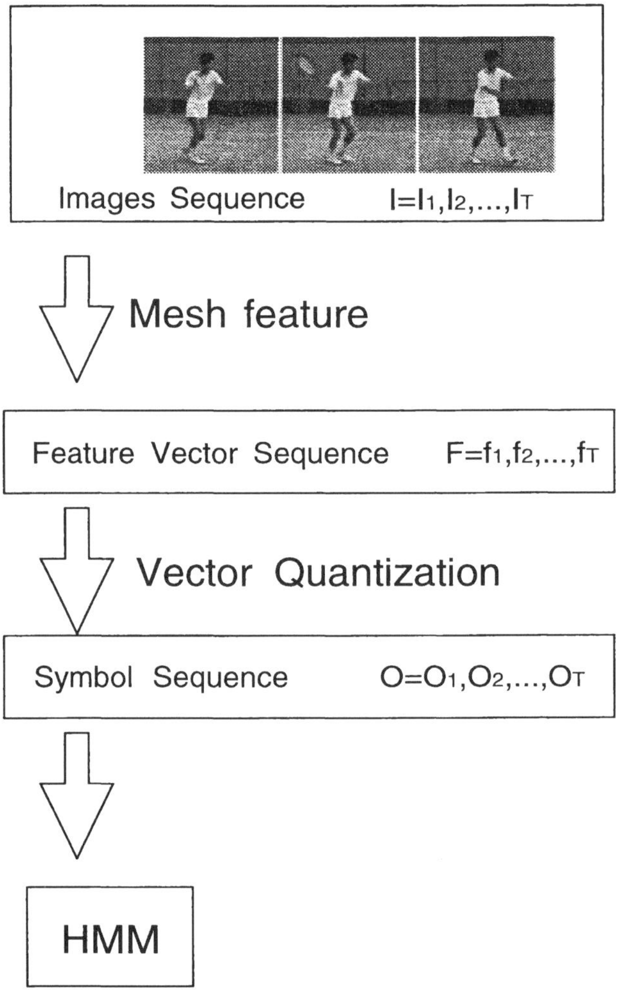

Figure 4.2. Processing flow

Each feature vector f_i is transformed into the symbol that is assigned to the codeword nearest the vector in the feature space. That means f_i is transformed to symbol v_j, if $j = \arg\min_j d(f_i, g_j)$ ($d(x, y)$: distance between x and y).

Image I_i is transformed into the symbol that is assigned to the codeword nearest feature vector f_i, and $O_i (= v_j)$ is yielded.

We used mesh feature [Umeda, 1982] as the feature vectors because they were successfully applied to complex-shaped 2D patterns such as multi-font characters. Figure 4.3 shows the calculation of the mesh features. Each binarized image ($M_I \times N_I$ pixels) is divided into $M_M \times N_M$ pixel meshes. The ratio of the black area becomes an element of the feature vector,

$$f(i,j) = number\ of\ black\ mesh(i,j)/(M_M \times N_M) \tag{4.14}$$

Thus, the feature vector sequence F extracted from an image sequence I is transformed to a symbol sequence O by applying mesh feature and vector quantization to each frame of a time-sequential image.

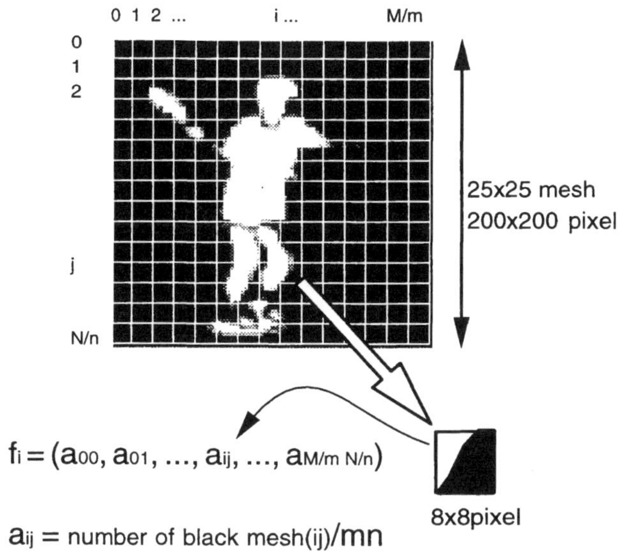

Figure 4.3. Mesh feature

These transformations have the advantage of being applicable to various images without manual tuning. This is because after extracting the human area, this method uses no parameters except mesh size, which can be determined from the size of the human.

As described in Section 4.2, the symbol sequences obtained by the above procedures are used for the recognition and learning phases. In recognition, the symbol sequence O obtained from an observed image sequence is substituted into Eqs. (4.1)-(4.5), and the recognition result is obtained as the category C^* that maximizes Eq. (4.5). In learning, the symbol sequences are obtained from training time-sequential image data, and the HMM's parameters are optimized for each category by Eqs. (4.11)-(4.13).

4.4. Experiments

4.4.1. Experimental conditions and pre-processes

We tested our algorithm on real time-sequential images. In our experiment, tennis actions were used as examples of human behaviors. The catetories to be recognized were six tennis actions: 'forehand stroke,' 'backhand stroke,' 'forehand volley,' 'backhand volley,' 'smash,' and 'service.'

Three persons performed each of the six tennis actions 10 times. The performances were captured by a TV camera (NTSC, 30 frames/second) and digitized into 200×200 pixel, 256 gray-level images. Figure 4.4 shows an original image sequence of the tennis action 'forhand volley,' where every fourth frame is displayed.

Preprocessing flow {

1) Preparing background image (Figure 4.5-(b)) for its original action images (Figure 4.5-(a)).

2) Blurring both images with a low pass filter (Figure 4.5-(d), (e)).

3) Extracting human area (Figure 4.5-(f)) with the following conditions:

if $|I_a(x,y) - I_b(x,y)| < th$;

$I_e(x,y) = 0$

else

$I_e(x,y) = I_a(x,y)$

I_e: human extracted image, I_a: original image

I_b: background image, th: threshold

}

Figure 4.4. Sample image sequence

In 2), blurring is performed to remove noise edges that remain in the background and could cause failure in human extraction. Compare Figure 4.5-(f) with Figure 4.5-(c), which is the difference image obtained by operation 3) without blurring operation 2).

Figure 4.6 is the human extracted images of Figure 4.4. We then binarized the extracted images so that white and black pixels corresponded to human areas

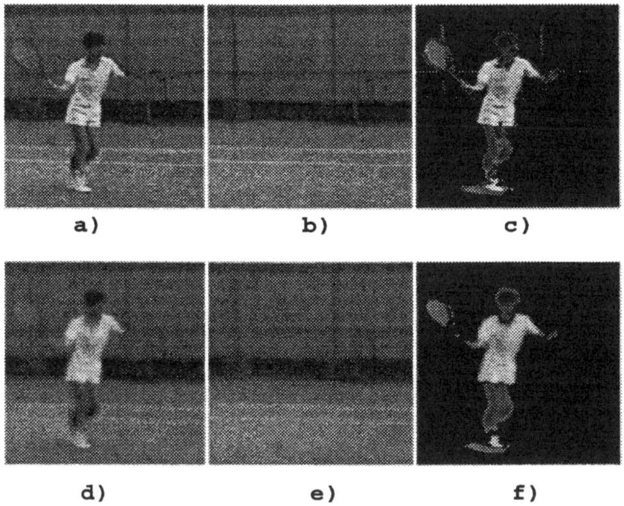

Figure 4.5. Extraction of human region

and background, respectively. Figure 4.7 shows binarized image examples of the six tennis actions.

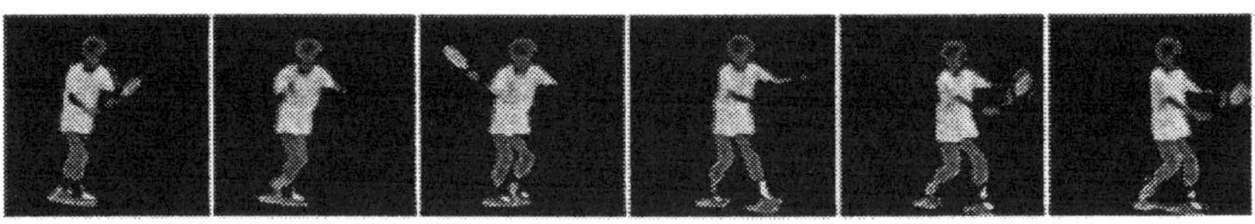

Figure 4.6. Extracted human images

The mesh feature extraction described in Section 4.3 is carried out for the binarized images. The size $M_M \times N_M$ of the mesh feature vector f_i in Eq. (4.14) was 8×8 pixels; consequently, the dimension n of f_i was 625. As the positions and sizes of human areas varied in the binarized images, the mesh center is placed at the center of gravity of each human area to avoid the influence of gross body displacement, or in other words, to normalize the positions. The sizes of humans were also normalized by scaling each frame of the binarized images so as to equalize the mean radii of human areas.

In the HMMs used in our experiment, the number N of states Q was set to 36. As the durations of the performances are not constant, the length of the

Figure 4.7. Target tennis actions

observed symbol sequences varied between 23 and 70. In training the HMMs, while the likelihood converged after about 100 iterations, we performed 150 iterations for each HMM.

4.4.2. Experiment 1

4.4.2.1 Experimental conditions. Experiments of recognizing actions of a person by the HMMs trained by the data of the same person were conducted for three subjects (Persons A, B and C). In each of the six actions, five sequences out of the 10 trials were used for learning, and the remaining five sequences were used for recognition tests.

4.4.2.2 Results. The recognition results are shown in Table 4.1 and Table 4.2. Table 4.1 shows the likelihood of 'forehand volley' with six HMMs trained with the data of Person C. The likelihood of the correct category is the highest.

Table 4.2 shows the recognition rates of all three persons with 10 different combinations of five training sequences out of the 10 trials; that is, for each person, there are 300 ($= 10 \times 5 \times 6$) test data. The average of the three persons was 96.0%.

Table 4.3 shows examples of symbol sequences: for training and testing, success and failure. Underlined symbols are those that do not appear in training patterns. It was confirmed that even though some symbols were inadequately assigned, action recognition by the patterns as a whole is robust.

Recognition performance worsens as the number of training patterns decreases. We also tested the recognizer constructed by HMMs trained by three training patterns in ten combinations. For one combination, the recognition rate was 100% (42/42) but for some other combinations it was not so good (78.5%).

Therefore, the performance of recognition system is dependent not only on the number of training patterns but also on how well the training patterns represent the category. When the number of training patterns is small, the recognition rate becomes more unstable. This is because the HMM parameters are critically dependent on the selection of training patterns.

To construct a robust recognition system, appropriate training patterns are important. This means training patterns should cover the maximum test pattern scatter possible. If covering the scatter with one HMM is difficult, we should divide the category into sub-categories.

4.4.3. Experiment 2

4.4.3.1 Experimental conditions. In experiment (2), learning and testing are completly separated. HMMs were trained with the sequences of one or two subjects and tested with the other subjects. HMMs for each category were trained by 10 mixed data sets of one or two subjects and tested with another person's data.

In this experiment, learning subjects and recognition subjects were separated not only in HMM processing but also in vector quantization. The code book of vector quantization was constructed by using only training data. This experiment is more appropriate for estimating the usefulness of this method in real situations because a real world recognition system should be person-independent. To achieve this, many people's data must be collected for learning. This reduced-scale experiment used mixed training data from more than one person to recognize another person's actions.

4.4.3.2 Results. In experiment (2), as shown in Table 4.4, the recognition rate of the HMMs that were trained with another subject's data were not as good as recorded in experiment (1). This is because test pattern subjects and training pattern subjects are different. Each person has some uniqueness in his action, but the variance range is limited in such a way that humans can recognize it. Thus we can improve the recognition rate by using mixed training data. The recognition rate of the HMMs trained with the data of two subjects was improved to 70.8%. Thus performance can be improved by collecting more training patterns that are suitable for representing the category.

Table 4.1. Likelihood (backhand volley)

HMM	log-likelihood
backhand volley (correct)	-29.8715
backhand stroke	-431.7681
forehand volley	-233.9752
forehand stroke	-442.1949
smash	-221.7908
serve	-466.5597

Table 4.2. Recognition rate (experiment 1)

Player	rate (%)
player A	90.66 (272/300)
player B	97.33 (292/300)
player C	100.00 (300/300)
Average	96.00

Table 4.3. Training patterns and test patterns

Learning	0 0 0 0 0 1 1 1 1 1 1 1 1 2 2 2 2 2 2 2 3 3 3 3 3 3 3 3 3 3 3 4 4 4 4 4 4 5 5 5 5 6 6 6 6 7 7 7 7 8 8 9 9 9 10 10 10 10 10 10 11 11 11 11 11 11
	1 1 1 1 1 1 1 1 1 1 32 2 2 2 2 2 2 2 3 3 3 3 3 3 3 3 3 3 3 3 3 3 4 4 4 5 5 5 6 6 6 6 6 7 7 7 8 8 9 9 9 10 10 10 10 11 11 11 11 11
	1 1 1 1 1 1 1 1 32 32 32 32 2 2 29 29 2 2 35 35 3 3 3 3 3 3 3 3 3 3 3 3 3 3 3 4 4 4 5 5 0 6 6 6 6 6 7 7 7 7 9 9 9 9 10 10 10 11 11 11 11
Test (Success)	1 1 32 33 32 32 32 32 32 33 28 28 28 28 28 29 29 2 35 35 35 35 3 3 3 3 3 3 3 3 35 3 3 3 3 3 3 3 4 4 32 35 0 0 5 5 6 6 6 6 7 7 8 8 8 9 9 10 10 10 11 11 11 11
	32 32 33 28 28 28 28 28 28 27 27 28 28 28 28 28 28 27 53 53 53 53 53 53 53 53 53 53 53 53 3 3 3 3 3 35 32 32 35 35 0 0 5 4 5 4 5 5 5 7 7 8 9 10 10 10 10 11 11 11 11
Test (Failure)	32 53 53 28 28 28 27 27 27 27 27 27 27 27 27 27 27 27 26 26 26 26 26 26 26 26 26 53 53 53 53 53 53 53 3 3 3 31 31 35 35 0 5 5 5 5 5 7 7 7 8 9 9 10 10 10 11 11 46 46 47
	53 53 53 27 27 27 27 27 27 27 27 27 26 26 26 26 26 26 26 26 26 26 26 26 26 26 26 13 13 13 13 13 26 13 53 53 53 53 53 53 53 2 2 2 3 3 3 3 3 3 4 4 4 5 5 7 7 7

Training patterns are 3 sequences, test (success) patterns are two sequences from three, and test (failure) patterns are two from four. Underlined symbols are not included in learning patterns. These examples shows that this method is robust to time-scale variance.

Table 4.4. Recognition rate (%) (experiment 2)

	Training data player			
Test data player	A	B	A+B	C
C	61.2	66.8	70.8	100.0

4.5. Category-separated vector quantization

4.5.1. Problem in VQ

The resulting recognition rate described in the previous section was not high enough for the subject other than the one used for training HMMs. The problem of implementation was mainly in the VQ stage because some missed samples described in Table 4.3 showed that they have many symbols that do not belong to the correct behavior category. To solve this problem, we introduced a new VQ configuration that we called category-separated VQ.

4.5.2. Category-separated VQ

We introduced "Category-separated" VQ (CSVQ) to improve the accuracy of the VQ stage. Figure 4.8 shows the concept of CSVQ. A VQ code book generated from all categories of training data is used in the conventional method. We used one code book for each class, or each HMM. The code book was generated from training data that belong to the class. All symbols from the CSVQ belong to the correct category, and this prevents miss-quantization. On the other hand, this causes overestimation of the likelihood for samples from different classes without giving any consideration to the distance from the prototype to the feature vector. Figure 4.9 explains the problem. The dimensionality of the feature space was very large compared to the number of the code words in a code book. In such space, many regions, which correspond to VQ code words, are not closed by others. In such an open region, a feature vector that is very far from the code word can be mathed with a code word. We used a penalty function, which is a gaussian distribution for the average class for all code words, to compensate the overestimation.

We used the LBG clustering algorithm [Linde et al., 1980] to generate a code book for the vector quantization. The LBG algorithm is based on recursive splitting k-mean clustering. We generate 32 clusters for each category of action. Figure 4.10 shows an example of a code book generated from the LBG algorithm. This demonstrates that all typical postures in a sequence of behavior are represented by the prototypes in the codebook.

We also improved the configuration of the HMMs. Left-to-right HMM (LR-HMM) is suitable for one-directional phenomena such as human behaviors. The LR-HMM has a restriction in state transition, and this reduces the number of parameters to be estimated. Accordingly, this improves the accuracy of parameter estimation with a restricted amount of training data.

4.5.3. Experiment

In this experiment, we evaluated the effect of CS-VQ using the same tennis actio image sequences used in the previous section.

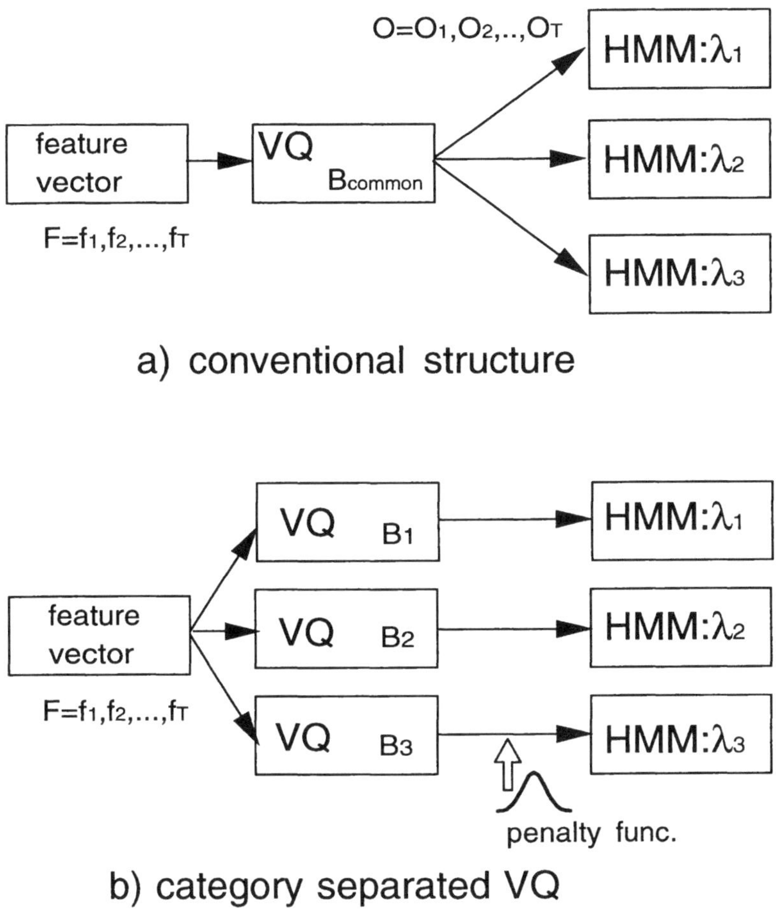

Figure 4.8. Category separated VQ

The Graphs in Figure 4.12 compares the recognition rate of the method described in the previous section with that of the metod in this section. The recognition rate improved in all conditions. This improvement has three factors: CS-VQ, LR-HMM, and the LBG algorithm. To separate the effect of CS-VQ, we compared one VQ code book version of LR-HMM and the LBG method, described as conventional method-2 in the graph in Figure 4.13. This demonstrates that CS-VQ improved the recognition rate by almost 90% even for a subject other than the one used in training the HMMs, while using three subjects for training.

In this section, we introduced CS-VQ to reduce recognition error, especially in the VQ stage. This method was successful in improving the recognition rate, but the CS-VQ is not only good for human behavior recognition. It was ap-

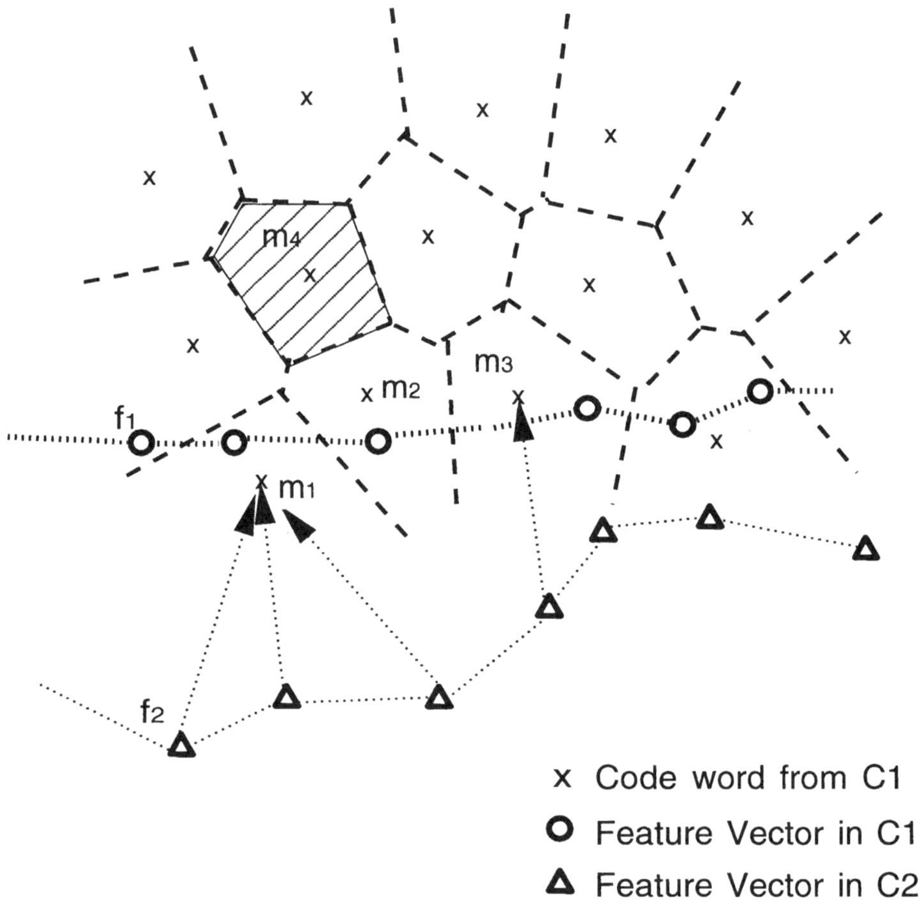

Figure 4.9. Feature vector sequence in feature space

plied to recognition of facial expression [Sakaguchi et al., 1995] and improved performance.

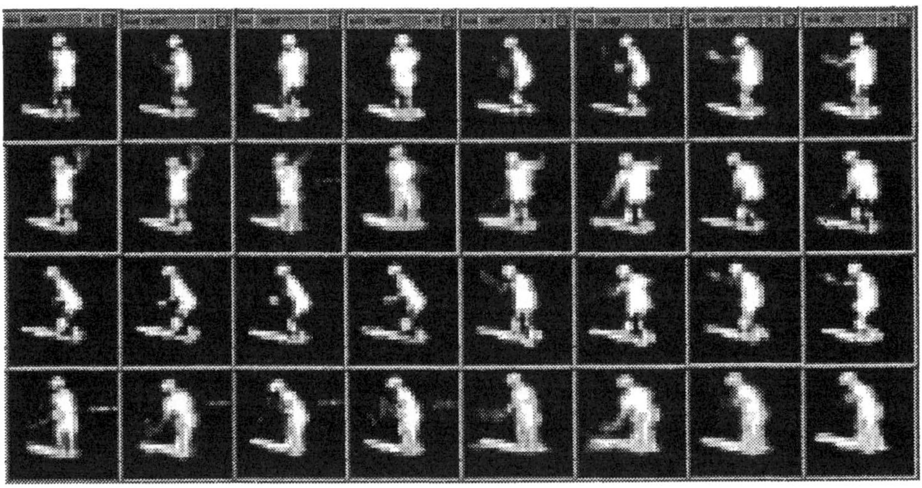

Figure 4.10. Code book generated from LBG Algorithm

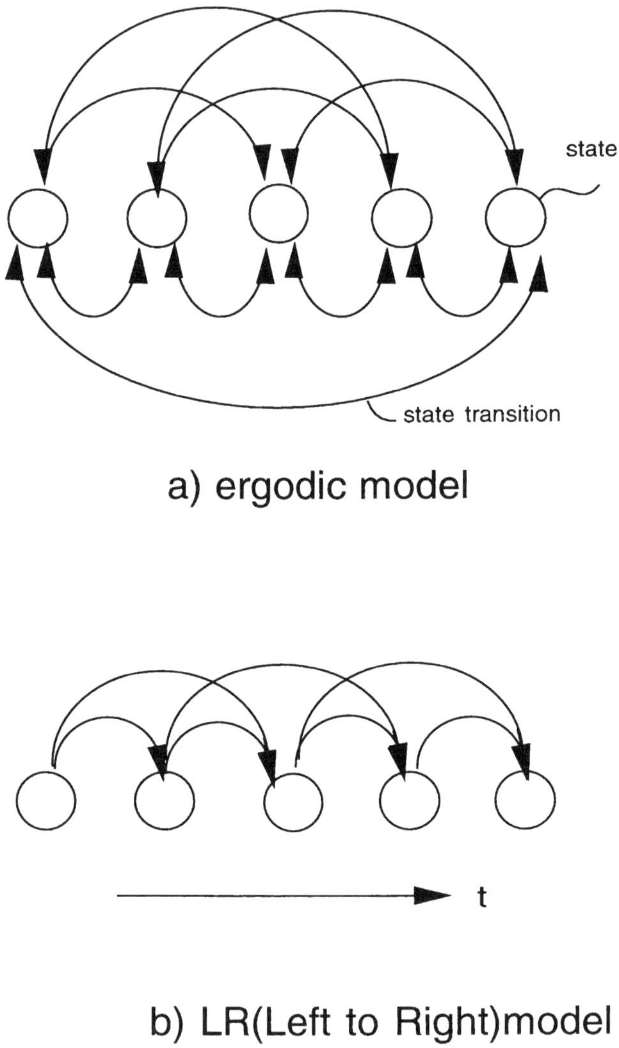

Figure 4.11. Ergodic HMM and LR HMM

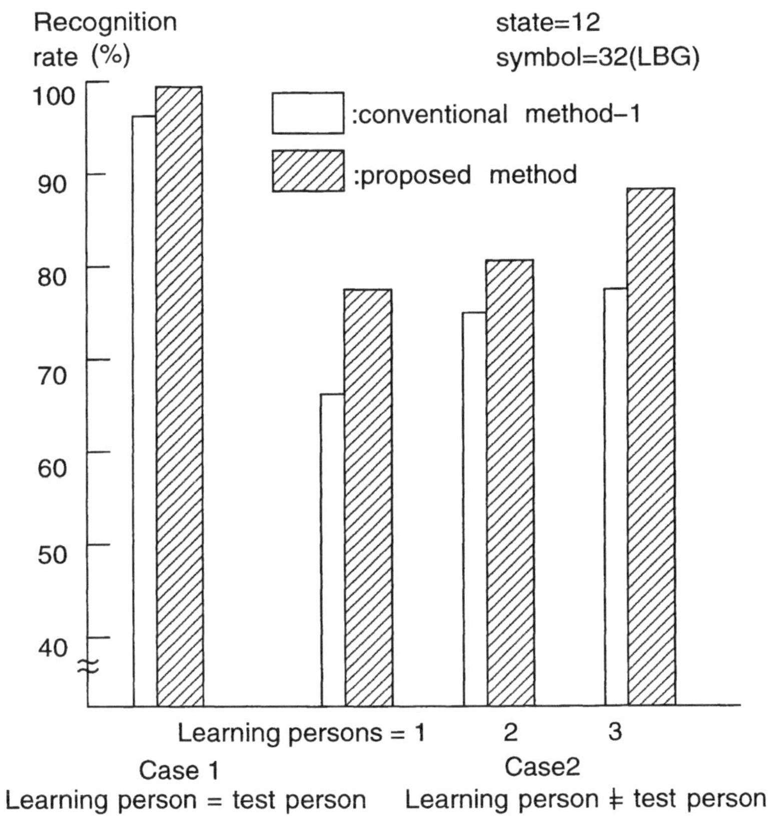

Figure 4.12. Recognition rate (1)

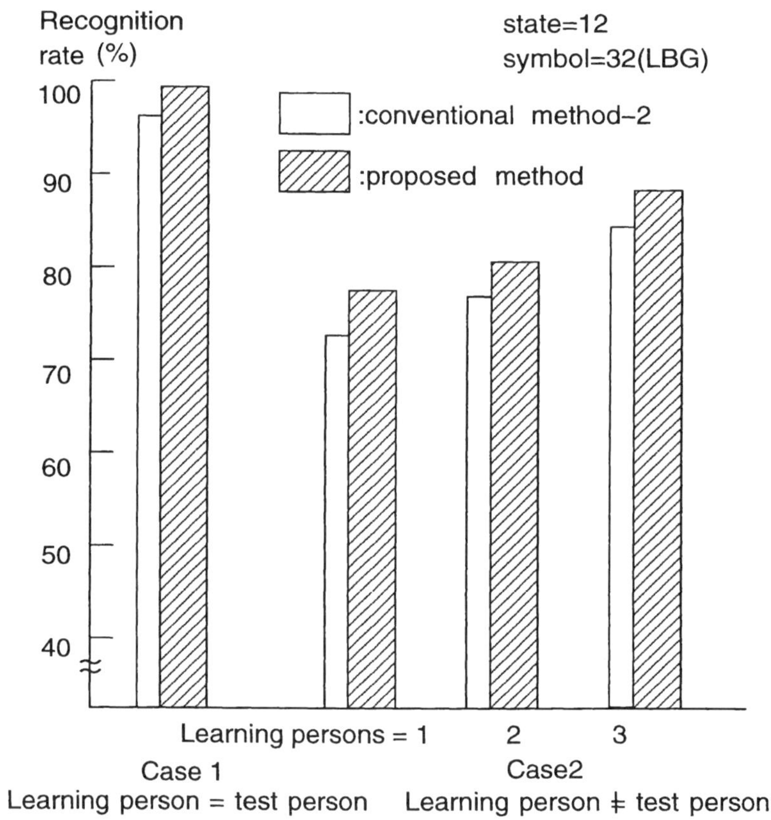

Figure 4.13. Recognition rate (2)

4.6. Applying Image Database Search

In this section, we describe an application of the behavior recognition method to content-based image database retrieval.

4.6.1. Process overview

The key point is that the discrete cosine transform (DCT) coefficient of the extracted image area is used as a feature vector. DCT is used in image compression standards such as JPEG and MPEG, and this implies that MPEG or JPEG compressed image data can be searched without decoding to the original image sequences. This is an advantage of the method. The target image sequences are compressed by MPEG1. Usually, MPEG data consists of three picture types: I, P, and B pictures. In this section, we did not use motion information and used only the I picture, which represents intra-frame coded picture. To evaluate the feasibility of the proposed method, we generated MPEG data where all frames are I picture and built a database for searching.

Figure 4.14 shows the processing flow of the method.

The target MPEG data consists of grayscale images, not the binarized images used in previous sections. All images were preprocessed, and human area extraction and positoin normalization were used. DCT coefficients for each 8x8 pixel block were extracted from this MPEG data, I, in the initial stage of decoding process. The lower frequency portions of these DCT coefficients for all blocks in an image, were used as a feature vector for an image frame. Figure 4.15 shows how the coefficients were chosen. From the upper-left corner, coefficients were zig-zag scanned to use x and y conponents evenly. The dimensionality of the feature vector equals the number of blocks in an image multiplied by the number of coefficients extracted from one block. The MPEG data is converted to a sequence of feature vectors. Then the sequence of feature vectors is converted into a symbol sequence. The HMMs are trained by the symbol sequences, and they recognize the sequences.

4.6.2. Experiment 1: Evaluation of DCT

In experiment 1, we evaluated the DCT coefficients as a feature vector. In the previous section, we used the mesh-feature for binarized images, but we cannot expect that a video database has a binarized human area. Here, the DCT coefficients for grayscale human images were evaluated as a feature vector for behavior recognition. The experimental conditions were the following: six categories of tennis actions, 200x200-pixel image sequences, 8bit grayscale, 12 states for LR-HMM, 16 code words for each category for CS-VQ, and 96 symbols for each HMM.

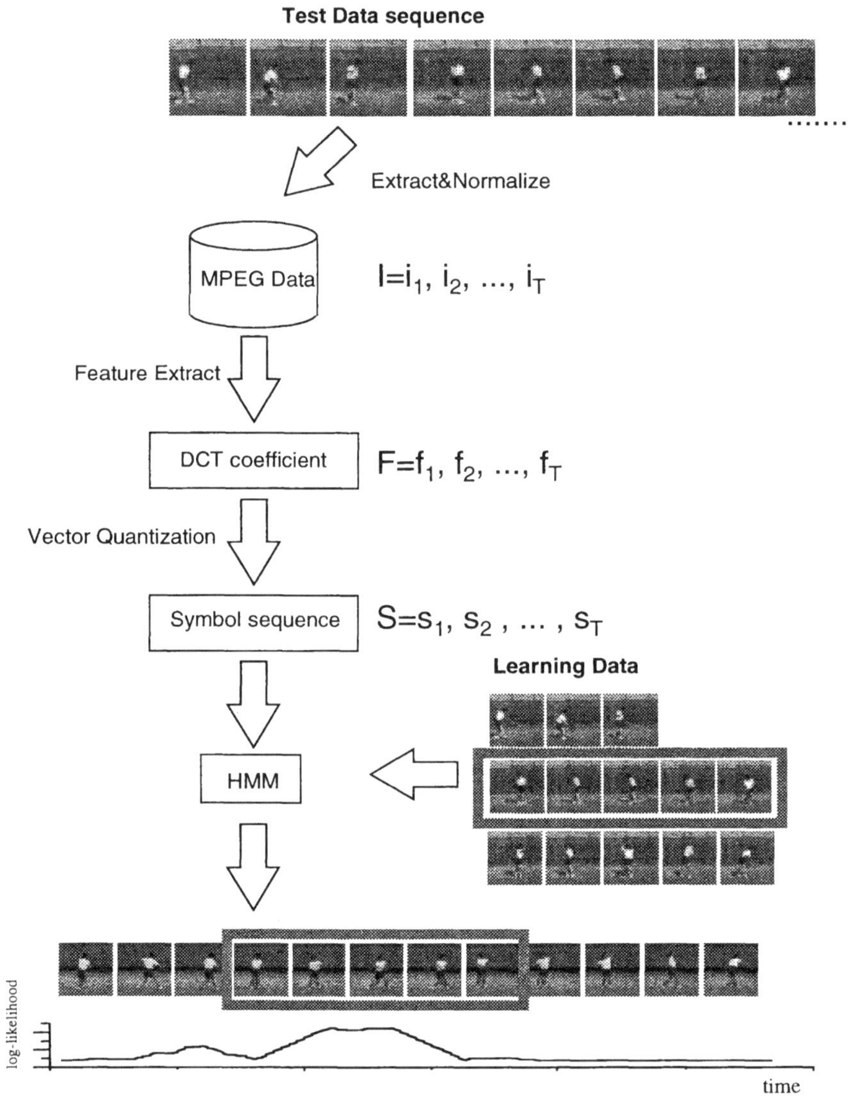

Figure 4.14. Processing flow of content-based image database retrieval using HMM behavior recognition method

We examined the performance of DCT coefficients for various sizes. The smallest one had one component, the upper-left corner DC component. The

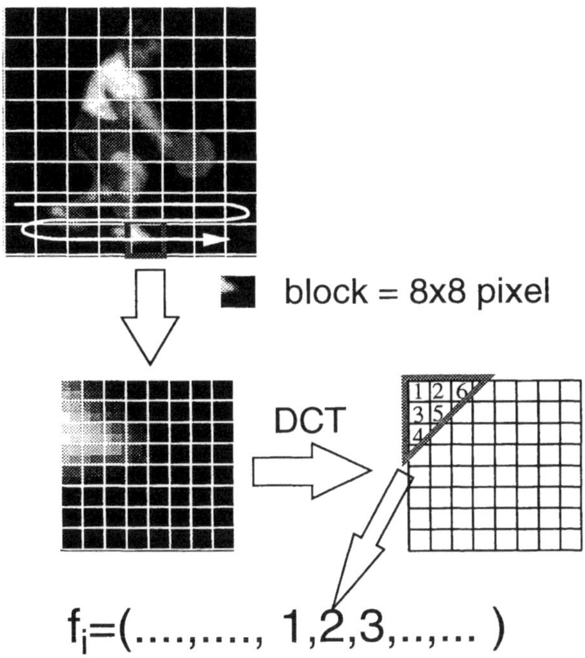

Figure 4.15. Extracting lower frequency portion of DCT coefficients

next one had three components from the first and second slanted row. Then, the zig-zag scanned DCT feature vectors that have 1, 3, 6, 10, 15, 21, and 28 components were examined. The more DCT coefficiets were used, the better performance for small images was expected. We used 16x16, 32x32, 64x64, and 128x128-pixel images for training and test data. These sizes were quantized by macro-block (16x16 pixels), which is a unit of a compression process in MPEG.

The recognition rate for each condition described above is shown in Figure 4.16. The sizes in the graph are described in macro-block size as a unit. The graph demonstrates that the recognition rate increases for a large number of DCT coefficients. The case of size one, DC component only, can be almost equivalent to the mesh feature. Even when the image is very small, e.g. 16x16 pixels, you can achieve over 98% recognition rate with 21 or 28 coefficients per block. As a result, DCT coefficients are suitable as a feature for behavior recognition with HMMs.

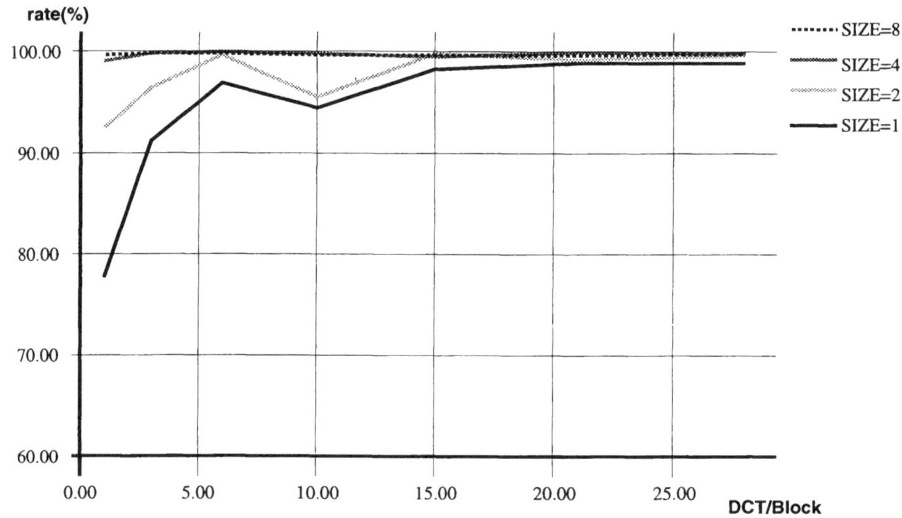

Figure 4.16. Recognition rates using DCT as a feature

4.6.3. Experiment 2: Evaluation of precision-recall

The performance of database retrieval is evaluated in this experiment. Figure 4.17 shows the log-likelihood of long video sequences that includes many behaviors. The graphs show log-likelihood for HMMs for six tennis behaviors. The log-likelihood is expected to become maximum at the end of a behavior. The graphs demostrate that each HMM becomes the maximum likelihood for its corresponding behavior. However, there may be some confusion. For example, the smash HMM shows a rather large likelihood for the backhand volley part of the video. In a recognition problem, the HMM that has maximum likelihood is chosen for the answer. Therefore, if the likelihood of the backhand volley HMM is larger than that of the smash HMM, there is no problem. However, in database retrieval, each behavior HMM has to processed independently. For example, when using simple thresholding, the threshold has to be less than all values for the correct HMMs and more than all values for the wrong HMMs. This is a much stricter requirement than in a recognition problem.

In this experiment, the performance for several threshold value were measured. The performance measures were a precision rate and a recall rate. The precision rate is the ratio of correct answer out of all retrieved ones. The recall rate is the ratio of actually retrievel answers out of all correct ones. These two ratios have a trade-off relationship. When the threshold is too large, a high precision rate can be achieved, but the recall rate becomes low. On the other hand, when the threshold is too small, the precision rate becomes low, while the recall rate can be high.

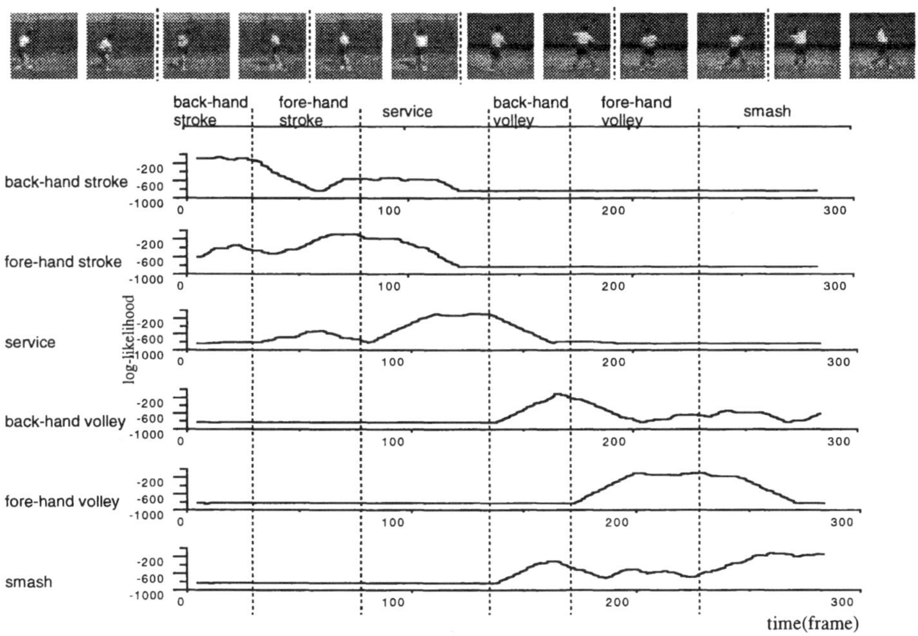

Figure 4.17. Spotting behaviors by thresholding log-likelihood

Figure 4.18 shows the precision rate and recall rate for six thresholding values; -100, -200, -300, -400, -500, and -600 in log-likelihood. From this graph, the optimal threshold is between -300 and -400, and about 80% for both rates can be achieved.

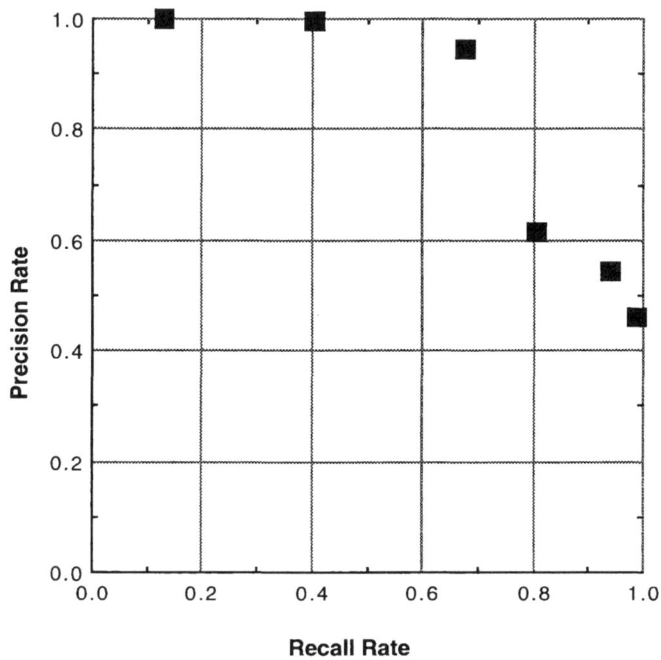

Figure 4.18. Precision rate and recall rate

The resulting 80% precision-recall is not enough for typical database retrieval. However, content-based image/video database are often used interactively; the database returns some results and the user check them and labels each result OK or NG. Then the system refines the search. In such interactive usage, this 80% precision-recall is presumably good enough for one step of query.

4.6.4. Extracting a moving area using an MC vector

In the method described above, we assumed that the preprocessing stage was achieved by some method, i.e., the moving human area in the image was extracted somehow. In behavior recognition applications, for example, survey-lance and monitoring, background subtraction can be used for human region extraction. However, for database retrieval, it is unrealistic to have to prepare background images. Moreover, the compressed image decoding in background subtraction can destroy the advantages of the method. Searching for compressed data without image decoding does have merits. Accordingly, one idea might be to use motion information and consider the moving region as a human region. Under this idea, it is reasonable to focus on the moving region to search the image database using human behaviors as a key. This idea has another advantage. MPEG data contains a motion compensation vector for each block. If this information can be used to extract the moving region, it can make compressed data decoding unnecessary for moving region extraction.

Based on this idea, a simple thresholding the size of MC is shown in Figure 4.19. The small boxes indicate blocks with large MC values, and the "+"s indicate small MC values. A human region is extracted approximately, but some noise does exist in the background region. Can such noise be eliminated by choosing the appropriate threshold? Unfortunately, the answer is no. In Figure 4.20, we gradually increase the threshold value from the upper-left figure to the lower-right figure. When all of the noise blocks are eliminated, the human region becomes too small to use.

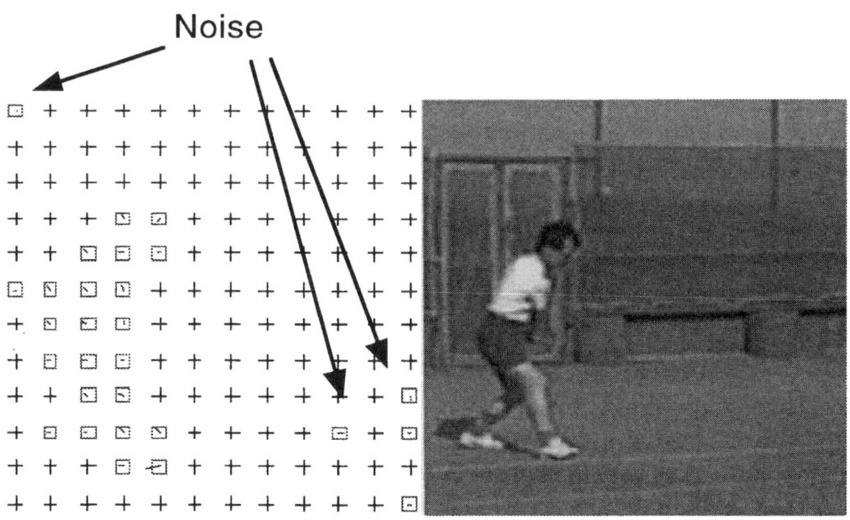

Figure 4.19. Moving area extraction using MC

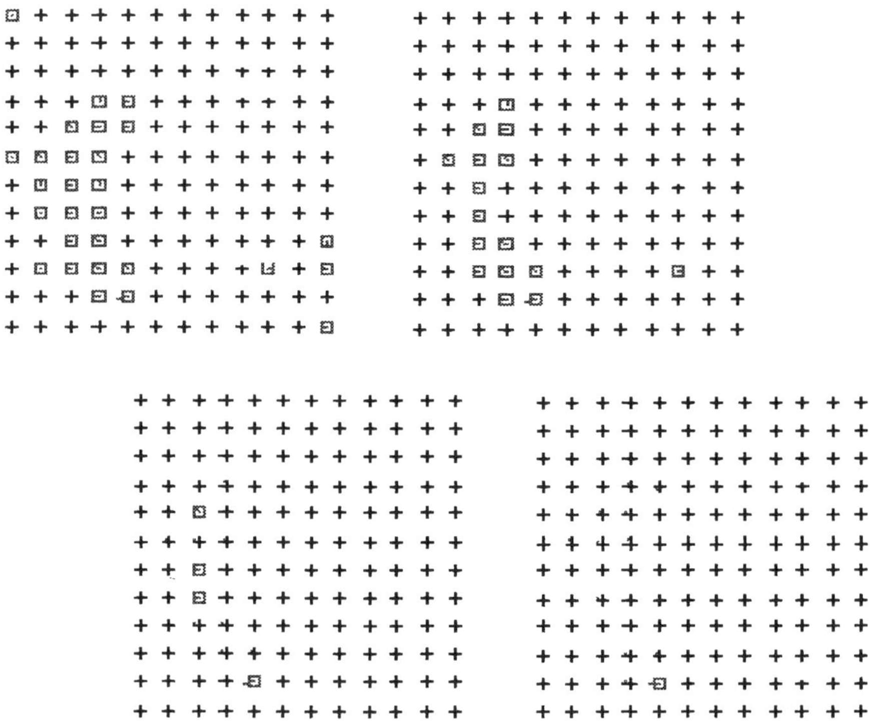

Figure 4.20. Moving area extraction using a simple threshold of MC.

The threshold value increases as follows: upper-left, upper-right, lower-left, and lower-right. When the threshold is large enough to eliminate all noise, the human region almost completely disappears.

To solve this problem, the characteristics of the noise blocks are important. Most "noise" blocks have weak textures. This problem is related to the mechanism of noise occurrence. Unfortunately, estimating the motion vectors for these blocks with weak textures is difficult. This is because they can easily match similar low textured blocks. For example, the ground region in the picture of Figure 4.19 has almost no texture, and can easily match to the other blocks in the ground. Accordingly, the certainty of the MC value is related to the texture of the block. The strength of the texture can be measured by the DCT coefficients of specific frequency band. Based on the above, we decided to use the combination of MC and DCT coefficients to eliminate all noise and obtain a stable moving region.

The block i is labeled as the moving region $\{$

if $MC_i > threshold_1$
else if $MC_i > threshold_2$ and $\sum_{j \in band} DCT_i(j) > threshold_{DCT}$
where $threshold_1 > threshold_2$, and the band is a specific frequency band of DCT.
}

This condition can successfully extract the human moving region without major noise in the background region. The resulting region is shown in Figure 4.21, where three consecutive frames are displayed. The middle frame is the same as Figure 4.19 and Figure 4.20. This demonstrates that the combination of MC and DCT enables the moving region to be extracted effectively.

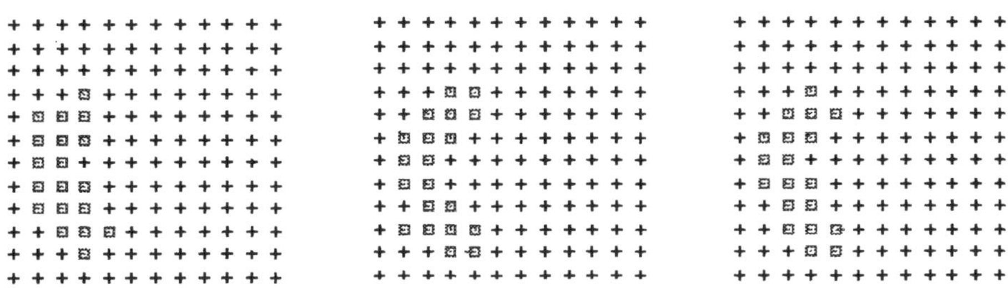

Figure 4.21. Extracted moving areas using a combination of MC and DCT.

4.7. Discussion and Conclusion

In this chapter, we discussed a human behavior recognition method using Hidden Markov Models and its application to image database retrieval. Using HMMs, human behaviors in a video sequence can be recognized with a simple and robust algorithm. A category-separated VQ was introduced to improve the performance with a rather small number of parameters to estimate. The application of HMMs to behavior recognition was initiated by the authors in the early 90's and is now widely used in this field[Cedras and Shah, 1995; Pentland, 2000]. There have been some state based approaches to the gesture recognition problems[Davis and Shah, 1994; Bobick and Wilson, 1997], and several extensions and modifications of HMM for behavior or sign language recognition[Brand et al., 1997; Brand, 1997]. Moreover, this method is becoming standard in human behavior recognition.

Notes

1. There are several types of HMMs according to the formulations used. In this chapter, we refer only to discrete HMMs that output symbol sequences. In continuous HMMs, which output continuous feature vectors, quantization error caused by the vector quantization procedure can be avoided, but the learning process is more complicated.

References

Aloimonos, J. (1990). Purposive and Qualitative Active Vision. In *Proceeding of ICPR*, pages 346–360.

Bobick, A. and Wilson, A. (1997). A state-based approach to the representaion and recognition of gesture. *IEEE Transaction on Pattern Analysis and Machine Intelligence.*

Brand, M. (1997). Couples hidden markov models for modeling interacting processes. Technical report, "The Media Lab, MIT".

Brand, M., Oliver, N., and Pentlan, A. (1997). Coupled hidden markov models for complex action recognition. In *Proceedings of the IEEE Conference on Computer Vision and Pattern Recognition.*

Cedras, C. and Shah, M. (1995). Motion Based Recognition: A Survey. *Image and Vision Computing*, 13(2):129–155.

Davis, J. and Shah, M. (1994). Visual Gesture Recognition. *Vision, Image and Signal Processing*, 141(2):101–106.

He, Y. and Kundu, A. (1991). Planar Shape Classification using Hidden Markov Model. In *Proc. CVPR'91*, pages 10–15.

Hogg, D. (1983). Model-based vision: a program to see a walking person. *Image and vision computing*, 1(1):5–20.

Horowitz, B. and Pentland, A. (1991). Recovery of Non-Rigid Motion and Structure. In *Proc. CVPR'91*, pages 325–330.

Huang, X. D., Ariki, Y., and Jack, M. A. (1990). *Hidden Markov Models for Speech Recognition.* Edinburgh Univ. Press.

Kunda, A., He, Y., and Bahl, P. (1989). Handwritten Word Recognition: a Hidden Markov Model Based Approach. *Pattern Recognition*, pages 283–297.

Linde, Y., Buzo, A., and Gray, R. (1980). An Algorithm for Vector Quantization. *IEEE Trans. Commin.*, 28(1):84–95.

Mao, W. and Kung, S. (1990). An Object Recognition System Using Stochastic Knowledge Source and VLSI Parallel Architecuture. In *Proc. 10th ICPR*, pages 832–836.

O'Rouke, J. and Badler, N. (1980). Model-Based Image Analysis of Human Motion Using Constraint Propagation. *IEEE Trans. PAMI*, PAMI-2(6):522–536.

Pentland, A. (2000). Looking at People: Sensing for Ubiquitous and Wearable Computing. *IEEE Transctions on Pattern Analysis and Machine Intelligence*, 22(1):107–119.

Rabiner, R. and Juang, B.-H. (1986). An Introduction to Hidden Markov Models. *IEEE ASSP MAGAZINE*, pages 4–16.

Rimey, R. and Brown, C. (1990). Selective Attention as Sequential Behavior: Modeling Eye Movements with an Augmented Hidden Markov Model. In *Proc. DARPA Image Understanding Workshop*, pages 840–849.

Sakaguchi, T., Ohya, J., and Kishino, F. (1995). Facial expression recognition using hmms. *Television society*, 49(8):1060–1067.

Samaria, F. (1993). Face Segmentation for Identification using Hidden Markov Models. In *Proceedings of 4th British Machine Vision Conference.*

Samaria, F. and Fallside, F. (1993). Automated Face Identification using Hidden Markov Models. In *Proceedings of the International Conference on Advanced Mechatronics.*

Terzopoulos, D. and Metaxas, D. (1991). Dynamic 3D Models with Local and Global Deformations: Deformable Superquadrics. *IEEE Trans. on PAMI*, 13(7):703–714.

Umeda, M. (1982). Recognition of Multi-Font Printed Chinese Characters. In *Proc. 6th ICPR*, pages 793–796.

Yamamoto, M. (1991). Human Motion Analysis Based on A Robot Arm Model. In *Proc. CVPR'91*, pages 664–665.

Yamato, J., Ohya, J., and Ishii, K. (1992). Recognizing Human Action in Time-Sequential Images using Hidden Markov Models. In *Proc. CVPR'92*, pages 379–387.

Chapter 5

CONCLUSION AND FUTURE WORK

Jun Ohya
Waseda University
Global Information and Telecommunication Institute
Bldg. 29-7, 1-3-10 Nishi-Waseda, Shinjuku-ku, Tokyo 169-0051, Japan

This book presents multiple persons' tracking , posture estimation, and behavior recognition as three core technologies in analyzing human images from video sequences. Each core technology is summarized as follows.

1 For tracking multiple persons regardless of occlusions, a multiple camera system based on non-synchronous observations is developed. This method utilizes a Kalman filtering based algorithm that updates tracking models for every observation so that temporally dense observations can be obtained. Experimental results show the effectiveness of the proposed method as well as the fact that the system is robust against changes in the number of cameras and the performance difference among observation nodes.

2 A real-time method for estimating the 3D coordinates of significant points on the human body from trinocular images is developed. This method utilizes a function that analyzes contour curvature of the human silhouettes so that each significant point is automatically located in each of the trinocular images without using heuristic rules and empirical knowledge about the human body, which were used in our earlier systems. Self-occlusions are dealt with by exploiting a Kalman filter based tracking algorithm and subtraction image processing. Good results for reproducing the estimated posture data in avatars in real-time were obtained in avatar based telecommunication systems.

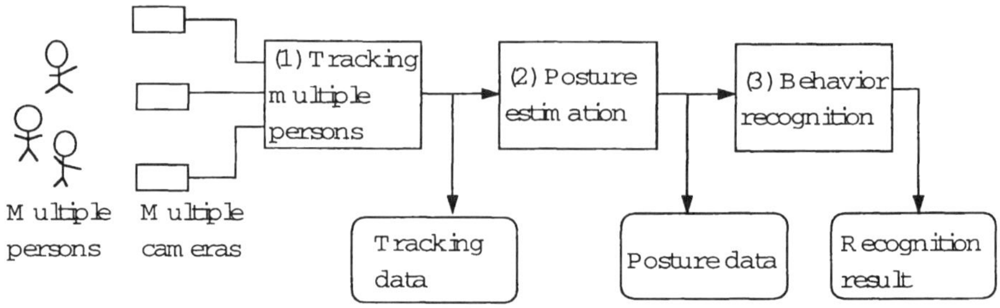

Figure 5.1. Tracking, Posture Estimation and Behavior Recognition

3 A method for recognizing human behaviors from time-sequential images using HMM (Hidden Markov Models) is presented. In this method, an image feature sequence is obtained from an original video sequence. Then, the image feature sequence is converted to a symbol sequence using Vector Quantization. In the learning mode, the model parameters of HMM are optimized so as to best describe training sequences. For recognition, the model that best matches the observed sequence is chosen. Some modifications are made for the vector quantization process and HMM configuration. Experimental results support the proposed method.

There are still some remaining issues to be solved in the future. We should integrate the three core technologies so that the system illustrated in Fig. 5.1 will be achieved. For this integration, since human body silhouettes are used by all the three core technologies, a more robust and general silhouette extraction method, which does not require uniform colored backgrounds, needs to be developed. In Fig. 5.1, technologies for interfacing mutiple persons' tracking and posture estiamtion and for interfacing posture estimation and behavior recognition are possibly a new issue to address. In the posture estimation module, a method for estimating postures of multiple persons based on the results of tracking multiple persons should be studied. In the behavior recognition, 3D posture estimation data should be combined with the image features so that more reliable recognition results can be achieved.

The remaining issues for each core technology are listed below.

- Tracking multiple persons

  - The calculations should be optimized by selecting the optimal cameras at each point in time and scheduling the image acquisitions using the Kalman filter's predictions of body positions.

- The current system uses only horizontal observations. Cameras from different view points such as from the top should be utilized as well.
- Optimization for camera arrangements depending on the environments (e.g., the shape of the room) should be studied.
- An efficient method for calibrating multiple cameras should be developed.
- Humans could interact with objects in the scene, and the system should be able to deal with this kind of interactions.

■ Posture estimation

- A method for dealing with occlusions in which a body part is occluded by other parts should be developed.
- In addition to the silhouette based features, some other information should be utilized to deal with self-occlusions.

■ Behavior recognition

- The number of categories to be recognized should be increased.
- The method should be improved so as to be able to recognize any person's behaviors.

Index

Baum-Welch algorithm, 104
DCT, 121
HMM, 102
Hidden Markov Models, 99, 101
JPEG, 121
Kalman filter, 7–8, 12, 15–16, 20, 70, 73
Kalman gain matrix, 76
Kalman gain, 14
LBG algorithm, 114
Left-to-right HMM, 114
MAP estimation, 13
MPEG, 121
Mahalanobis distance, 26
Spatial redundancy, 10
Temporal Redundancy, 11
Vector Quantization, 101
Anatomy for artists, 90
Appropriateness, 66
Autoregressive model (AR model), 70, 73
Background region, 23
Border tracking, 49
Calibration, 46
Center of gravity, 47
Code book, 114
Color, 23
Contour, 49, 70–71
Covariance matrix, 76
Database retrieval, 124
Difference image, 70
Discrete HMMs, 130
Discrete cosine transform (DCT), 88
Distance transformation, 23, 47
Distributed processing, 15
Dynamic systems, 12
Elbow, 52–53, 65
Facial expression, 87
Feature extraction, 23
Feature space, 105
Feature vector, 105
Forward algorithm, 104
Front image, 77
Function analysis, 70–71
Genetic algorithm (GA), 52, 65
Image difference, 73, 76
Implementation, 22
Infrared camera, 46
Intensity, 23
Knee, 52–53, 65
Learning, 52, 65
Likelihood, 104
Linear system, 12–13
Magnetic sensor, 44
Measurement error, 12, 18, 20
Mesh feature, 101, 106
Multiple cameras, 60
Multiple-camera system, 15
Mutual occlusion, 9
Network, 26
Non-synchronous observations, 15–16
Occlusion, 66
Occlusions, 7
Physical properties, 19
Pixel value, 23
Posture estimation, 44
Posture parameter, 44
Posture, 43
Precision rate, 125
Principal axis (PA), 61
Principal axis of upper body(PAU), 49
Recall rate, 125
Rotation angle of body, 61
Scalability, 8
Segmentation, 23
Self-occlusion, 7, 9, 70, 76
Sequential image, 23
Side image, 77
Significant point, 44, 49, 61, 70
Silhouette, 46, 49, 70
Skeleton, 50
State vector, 76
Stereo, 8
Stochastic image, 23
System throughput, 8
Temporal axis, 9
Temporary top of head, 50
Test pattern, 111–112
Thermal image, 46
Tip of foot, 50, 63

Tip of hand, 51, 65
Top camera, 61
Top image, 78
Top of head, 52, 63
Tracking algorithm, 20
Tracking, 73
Training patterns, 111–112
Transition matrix, 18
Upper half of body, 48
Viewpoint, 10
Virtual environment, 86
Virtual metamorphosis, 86
Vision system, 8